MW00764789

PRESENTED TO:

_____

BY:

_____

DATE:

_____

BE
LIKE
JESUS

BE
LIKE
JESUS

180
DEVOTIONS AND PRAYERS
FOR KIDS

MARILEE PARRISH

BARBOUR BOOKS
An Imprint of Barbour Publishing, Inc.

© 2019 by Barbour Publishing, Inc.

ISBN 978-1-68322-884-4

All rights reserved. No part of this publication may be reproduced or transmitted for commercial purposes, except for brief quotations in printed reviews, without written permission of the publisher.

Churches and other noncommercial interests may reproduce portions of this book without the express written permission of Barbour Publishing, provided that the text does not exceed 500 words or 5 percent of the entire book, whichever is less, and that the text is not material quoted from another publisher. When reproducing text from this book, include the following credit line: "From *Be Like Jesus: 180 Devotions and Prayers for Kids*, published by Barbour Publishing, Inc. Used by permission."

Unless otherwise indicated, all scripture quotations are taken from the New Life Version © 1969 and 2003 by Barbour Publishing, Inc. All rights reserved.

Scripture quotations marked AMP are taken from the Amplified® Bible, © 2015 by The Lockman Foundation. Used by permission.

Scripture quotations marked ESV are from The Holy Bible, English Standard Version®, © 2001 by Crossway Bibles, a publishing ministry of Good News Publishers. Used by permission. All rights reserved.

Scripture marked GNT taken from the Good News Translation® (Today's English Standard Version, Second Edition), © 1992 American Bible Society. All rights reserved.

Scripture quotations marked ICB are from The Holy Bible, International Children's Bible® © 1986, 1988, 1999, 2015 by Tommy Nelson™, a division of Thomas Nelson. Used by permission.

Scripture quotations marked MSG are from *THE MESSAGE.* © by Eugene H. Peterson 1993, 1994, 1995, 1996, 2000, 2001, 2002. Used by permission of NavPress Publishing Group.

Scripture quotations marked NIV are taken from the HOLY BIBLE, NEW INTERNATIONAL VERSION®. NIV®. © 1973, 1978, 1984, 2011 by Biblica, Inc.™ Used by permission. All rights reserved worldwide.

Scripture quotations marked NLT are taken from the *Holy Bible.* New Living Translation © 1996, 2004, 2015 by Tyndale House Foundation. Used by permission of Tyndale House Publishers, Inc. Carol Stream, Illinois 60188. All rights reserved.

Published by Barbour Books, an imprint of Barbour Publishing, Inc., 1810 Barbour Drive, Uhrichsville, Ohio 44683, www.barbourbooks.com

Our mission is to inspire the world with the life-changing message of the Bible.

Member of the
Evangelical Christian
Publishers Association

Printed in the United States of America.
06444   0318   BP

INTRODUCTION

Hello friends! What an adventure we're about to have! Knowing Jesus and learning to be like Him is the greatest adventure offered to us as humans. John 10:10 tells us that Jesus came to give us *abundant life*. What does that mean? Jesus said it this way: "I came that they may have *and* enjoy life, and have it in abundance [to the full, till it overflows]" (AMP).

Sounds like a great adventure to me! But it's also a choice that each of us is given when we first meet Jesus. We can choose to get to know Him and follow His ways of adventure and abundant life, or we can choose to turn away from Him and try to find life on our own.

In the pages ahead, we're going to take an in-depth look at the life of Jesus so that we can know who we are following. What you learn about Jesus and the life He offers might rock your world!

Your friend on the journey,
MariLee

WHO IS JESUS?

The much-loved Son is beside the Father. No man has ever seen
God. But Christ has made God known to us.

JOHN 1:18

To be like someone, we have to know who they are. So for us to learn
how to be like Jesus, we must get to know Him first! As we begin our
adventure together, here are some important things to know about Jesus:

- Jesus is the Son of God (Mark 1:1).
- Jesus came so that we could know God (John 1:18).
- Jesus came to save us from our sins so that we can live
  forever (John 3:16–17).
- Jesus is the image of the invisible God (Colossians 1:15).
- Jesus is the only way to God (John 14:6).
- Jesus loves you (John 15:9)!

Now, some of these facts about Jesus might be confusing. But that's
because God is *so big*, we can't possibly understand everything about Him.
But here's the amazing thing: whenever you have a question about Jesus,
you can just ask Him! Matthew 11:25 tells us, "Jesus said, 'I praise you,
Father, Lord of heaven and earth, because you have hidden these things
from the wise and learned, and revealed them to little children' " (NIV).

You are so special to Jesus. He wants to tell you things about Himself
that some adults can't even understand.

---

*Jesus, I'm so thankful that You want me to know who You are.
Please work in my heart as I learn more about You. Amen.*

JESUS LOVES YOU

The Lord came to us from far away, saying, "I have loved
you with a love that lasts forever. So I have helped
you come to Me with loving-kindness."

JEREMIAH 31:3

Look at these amazing verses that tell us how much Jesus loves us:

- "This is love! It is not that we loved God but that He loved us. For God sent His Son to pay for our sins with His own blood." (1 John 4:10)

- "But God showed His love to us. While we were still sinners, Christ died for us." (Romans 5:8)

- "No one can have greater love than to give his life for his friends." (John 15:13)

And that's just a few! God's Word is full of evidence that shows how much He loves each one of us—including *you*. Even if you've messed up more than you've ever messed up in your life, nothing will change the fact that God loves you. Nothing you can ever do will cause Him to love you any more or any less. Before we can begin to be like Jesus, we must accept His love for us and choose to follow Him. Are you ready to do that?

---

*Jesus, I accept Your love for me! I believe You died on
the cross to show me Your love and to take away all my sin.
Forgive me for my mistakes. I know I can't make good
choices without Your help. I choose to follow You.
Help me be like You, Jesus.*

JESUS IS ALL-POWERFUL

Jesus came and said to [His disciples], "All power has
been given to Me in heaven and on earth.... And I am
with you always, even to the end of the world."

MATTHEW 28:18, 20

God's Word tells us in many places that Jesus is all-powerful. Take a few
minutes and look up Ephesians 1:19–22. Before you read it, ask Jesus to
teach you something new that you've never understood before. If you've
put your trust in Jesus, you have great power available to you in every
moment. It's true that the very same power that raised Jesus from the
dead is the power that lives inside each of us who trust in Jesus. Isn't that
amazing? Jesus breathed His Holy Spirit into us to teach us the truth
(John 14:15–17), to help us when we're weak (Romans 8:26), to give us
gifts (1 Corinthians 12:1–11), to lead us (Romans 8:14), to convict us
(John 16:8), to give us wisdom (1 Corinthians 2:7–16), and to fill us with
power (Acts 1:8). God gave us the power of the Holy Spirit so that we
can learn to be like Jesus!

---

*God, thank You for putting the Holy Spirit right inside my
heart to lead me closer to Jesus. Help me learn to listen as
the Spirit speaks to my heart. Remind me of the great power
that lives inside me—a power that can change the world!*

JESUS WAS BAPTIZED

When Jesus came up out of the water, the heavens opened.
He saw the Spirit of God coming down and resting on
Jesus like a dove. A voice was heard from heaven. It said,
"This is My much-loved Son. I am very happy with Him."
MATTHEW 3:16–17

During our adventure, we're going to travel through the Gospels together
to learn how to be like Jesus. The first stop is the book of Matthew.
Matthew begins by telling us about the birth of Jesus. You already know
this story—it's all about Christmas! But starting in Matthew 3, we are
introduced to John the Baptist. He is preparing the way for Jesus to start
His ministry on earth. The first thing we see Jesus do when He starts
His ministry is get baptized. Have you seen people at church getting
baptized? Baptism is a public expression of what took place in our hearts
when we chose to follow Jesus. It shows others that we want to be like
Jesus! Ask Jesus if this is something He wants you to do soon. He'll
help you understand if the timing is right for you. Then check with your
parents and leaders at your church to discuss the details.

---

*Jesus, I want to be like You. Show me if being baptized is the next
step for me on this great adventure of learning to be more like You.
Help me have the courage I need to follow You. Amen.*

JESUS WAS TEMPTED

Jesus was led by the Holy Spirit to a desert. There He was tempted by the devil. Jesus went without food for forty days and forty nights. After that He was hungry. The devil came tempting Him and said, "If You are the Son of God, tell these stones to be made into bread." But Jesus said, "It is written, 'Man is not to live on bread only. Man is to live by every word that God speaks.'"

MATTHEW 4:1–4

After Jesus was baptized, He went to the desert and chose not to eat so He could focus on God for forty days and forty nights. Satan used that opportunity to try to get Jesus to sin. The Bible tells us that our enemy, Satan, is the father of lies. He will try every trick in the book to get you to mess up. What did Jesus do? He told Satan the truth from God's Word. When you feel like you are being tempted to make a bad choice, ask Jesus for help. He's been there! He knows how to help you overcome. When you memorize scripture, God will help you remember those powerful words at just the right time. Start with this one: "No temptation has overtaken you except what is common to mankind. And God is faithful; he will not let you be tempted beyond what you can bear. But when you are tempted, he will also provide a way out so that you can endure it" (1 Corinthians 10:13 NIV).

Jesus, when I'm tempted, help me remember Your words.

FISHERS OF MEN

Jesus said to [Simon Peter and Andrew],
"Follow Me. I will make you fish for men!"
MATTHEW 4:19

Jesus asks us to follow Him. But doing so is always our choice. He never demands that we choose Him; He invites us on an eternal adventure as His friend. Jesus met His first disciples beside the Sea of Galilee. They were fishermen. He called to them, and they chose to leave their jobs and follow Him. When we say yes to following Jesus, the adventure begins. Jesus didn't need these guys, but He wanted them. It's the same with us. He doesn't need us to follow Him and serve Him, but He loves us and wants us to be in relationship with Him. He wants to partner with us as we bring His kingdom together! What does "bring His kingdom" mean? It means that we get to share the love and life of Jesus with everyone He puts in our lives. It's not just telling others about Jesus; it's about living in a way that shows we believe in a God who loves us and cares about everything in our lives. Our actions speak a lot louder than our words.

---

*Jesus, I want to partner with You as we bring
Your kingdom to everyone around me. I'm so thankful
that You want to use me to do Your work!*

THE GOOD NEWS

Jesus went over all Galilee. He taught in their places of
worship and preached the Good News of the holy nation.
MATTHEW 4:23

Have you heard of the "Good News" before? The Bible often refers to the
"Good News" or the "Gospel." The Good News is that Jesus has come!
Listen in as Jesus tells you what this means: "The Spirit of the Lord is on
me, because he has anointed me to proclaim good news to the poor. He
has sent me to proclaim freedom for the prisoners and recovery of sight
for the blind, to set the oppressed free, to proclaim the year of the Lord's
favor" (Luke 4:18–19 NIV).

Jesus wasn't just saying that He came for people who didn't have
any money (although He definitely came for them too!). In the original
language that Jesus spoke, the word *poor* meant "afflicted, distressed,
hopeless." Have you ever felt hopeless? A lot of people did in Jesus'
time—and a lot of people feel that way today too. That's why the Good
News is so important!

Jesus came to bring hope to hopeless people! He came to bring
freedom and joy to people who have never known happiness. You're
going to run into a lot of people in your lifetime who need to know
where to find hope. Being like Jesus means sharing the Good News with
people who need it.

---

*Jesus, thank You for bringing Your kingdom to me and
to anyone who chooses to say yes to You. Help me to share
Your Good News with people who need it.*

HAPPY AND BLESSED

"Those who have a pure heart are happy,
because they will see God."
MATTHEW 5:8

The Bible talks a lot about being "blessed" and having joy. Joy and blessing come from being like Jesus! When Jesus talks about having joy, He's talking about a deep understanding that Jesus is with us and making everything right—no matter what. That means that even if you are having a really bad day, you can still have joy. Why? Because of this promise from God: "We know that in all things God works for the good of those who love him, who have been called according to his purpose" (Romans 8:28 NIV). God is with you, and He's working everything out for your good, even when things don't seem to be going your way at the moment. Even if your best friend is mad at you. Even if you're in trouble with Mom and Dad. Even if life seems completely beyond your control. As you learn to be more like Jesus, He'll continue to fill you with His kind of joy. And you'll be happy and blessed!

Jesus, I want to see You and learn to be like You. Please fill me with Your kind of joy no matter what kind of day I'm having. Help me to trust that You're working everything out for my good.

SIMPLY SHINE

"Let your light shine in front of men. Then they will
see the good things you do and will honor your
Father Who is in heaven."

MATTHEW 5:16

Want to know the best way to share the love of Jesus with others? Be You! Simply be the amazing person God created you to be! Are you an artist? Use that God-given talent and be the best artist you can be! Are you a good dancer? Shine the light of Jesus through your smile and your pure heart as you dance for Jesus. Are you good at singing or playing the piano? Shine for Jesus as you worship Him through your music. God gave each of us special gifts to use to glorify Him and show others how amazing He is! Not sure what gifts you have? Ask Jesus to show you the special gifts and talents that He put inside you. Ask your parents or other trusted grown-ups what makes you special. A lot of times, other people can see what's so special about us better than we can. Jesus wants you to know what makes you special! So go find out—and then use those special gifts to be more like Jesus.

---

*Jesus, I want to worship You with my gifts and talents,
but sometimes I'm not sure how. Can You show me? Please open
my eyes and heart to see the ways that You made me special.
Help me to be brave as I use these special gifts to be like You.*

WORDS MATTER

"Whoever says to his brother, 'You have no brains,'
will have to stand in front of the court."

MATTHEW 5:22

Do you have a brother or sister? Or maybe a cousin or close friend? Chances are you've gotten upset with them over something at some time. Maybe they were annoying you or not sharing the way you hoped they would. You might even have said something mean to them in the moment. Can you remember a time like that? This verse doesn't literally mean that you have to go to court if you tell your brother that he's dumb. But Jesus is telling us that our words matter. They reveal what's really going on in our hearts. If you've hurt someone with your words, the best thing to do is to talk to Jesus about it first and then go make it right with the person you hurt. Ask Jesus to give you His heart for your friend or relative. What does that mean? It means asking Jesus to show you how He feels about that person. Does Jesus love them? You bet He does. Does Jesus know what may have happened to cause that person to act in a certain way (maybe they had a bad day, maybe someone else hurt their feelings, maybe they had a tummy ache)? Of course He does. Being like Jesus means you are careful with your words.

Jesus, please help me be more careful with my words. Please give me the courage to go to the person I've hurt and tell them I'm sorry.

TELLING THE TRUTH

"Let your yes be YES. Let your no be NO."
MATTHEW 5:37

People lie and break promises all the time. Has someone ever told you a lie? It hurts, doesn't it? It makes you not want to trust that person anymore. Jesus wants His followers to be trustworthy. When you say you're going to do something, do it. Instead of always saying "I promise" to do something, simply show that you will by doing it. When you tell your brother that you'll give him a piece of candy if he shares his stickers with you, make sure you keep your word and do it. If you don't, he won't trust you next time and will be less likely to share with you.

Your parents want to trust you too. If you say that you're going to turn off your light right after you've read the next page, make sure you do what you say you're going to do. The more trustworthy you are, the more privileges and responsibilities you'll be given as you grow up!

Being like Jesus means you tell the truth and you do what you say you're going to do.

Jesus, I want people to trust me.
Help me to do what I say I'm going to do.

LOVING OTHERS

"If you say hello only to the people you like, are you doing any more than others? The people who do not know God do that much."

MATTHEW 5:47

Have you ever felt left out? It doesn't feel very good, does it? Jesus wants us to include others and be kind to them even if they don't happen to be our very best friends. Jesus says that even people who don't know God are kind to their friends. Being like Jesus means that you go above and beyond to be kind to others, not just your friends. Maybe there's a kid in your class that nobody likes and he or she is always sitting alone. Could Jesus give you the courage to go say "hello" with a smile? Yes, of course He can. You might even make a new friend and discover that you have a lot in common. Sometimes shy people sit alone because they're afraid. Can you pray for that person to feel loved and accepted? Yes! Love makes fear disappear (1 John 4:18). Isn't that amazing? And Jesus gives you the power to help other people who are afraid. That's pretty awesome!

Jesus, please fill me with Your power and courage to love others even when I don't feel like it—or when it might be embarrassing. Help me see others as You see them.

SURPRISE GIVING

"Your giving should be in secret. Then your Father
Who sees in secret will reward you."
MATTHEW 6:4

Everyone loves a good surprise! When was the last time you received a good surprise? How did it make you feel? Have you ever surprised someone else with a special gift? It's so fun to watch someone receive a gift that we made for them as a surprise. Jesus loves a good surprise too! In fact, He tells us that giving is best when it's done as a secret. Some people in Jesus' time were giving to be seen by other people. They weren't giving because they wanted someone else to feel special; they were giving so that they could feel more special about themselves. Jesus knows what's in our hearts. He knows our motives. That means He knows exactly what we're thinking. If we're giving a gift just so that other people will think better of us, that is not okay. Jesus wants us to give with pure hearts. When we give, we're not only blessing the receiver, but we're also blessing Jesus. Giving is an act of worship. Can you ask Jesus if there is someone in your life whom He would like you to surprise with a special gift?

*Jesus, I'm glad You know my thoughts. I want to worship You
by the things I think and do. Show me whom I can
bless with a special gift this week.*

SECRET PRAYERS

"When you pray, go into a room by yourself. After you have shut
the door, pray to your Father Who is in secret. Then your
Father Who sees in secret will reward you."

MATTHEW 6:6

Some people in Jesus' day would pray loud and long for all to hear. They
wanted others to feel badly about themselves while making their own
selves feel good and prideful. Jesus gave us a better example of how to
pray. He said to pray like this: "Our Father in heaven, Your name is holy.
May Your holy nation come. What You want done, may it be done on
earth as it is in heaven. Give us the bread we need today. Forgive us our
sins as we forgive those who sin against us. Do not let us be tempted,
but keep us from sin. Your nation is holy. You have power and shining-
greatness forever. Let it be so" (Matthew 6:9–13).

You can add whatever else you'd like to your prayers, but the
important thing is simply to pray to Jesus and tell Him what's on your
heart. He already knows everything about you, but He loves it when you
come to Him and talk to Him. Try picturing Jesus in your mind while
you pray. God loves it when you use your imagination as you talk to Him
because He created your imagination!

---

*Jesus, thank You for showing me how to be more like You.
Thank You for giving me a great imagination.*

TREASURE IN HEAVEN

"Gather together riches in heaven where they will not be eaten
by bugs or become rusted. Men cannot break in and steal them.
For wherever your riches are, your heart will be there also."

MATTHEW 6:20–21

Have you ever seen a movie in which people are hunting for buried treasure? Usually the people hunting the treasure become obsessed with the treasure and think it will meet all of their needs. Sometimes it's fun to pretend we're hunting for buried treasure, especially when playing at the beach. Jesus talks about gathering riches that can't ever be taken from us. Can you think of what He might mean? Is your family a treasure? Is your friendship with Jesus a treasure? Are love and joy things you can treasure? Of course! If we become obsessed with *things*, our hearts will never be content or happy. But when we treasure Jesus and the love He has put in our hearts, we will be blessed beyond measure!

---

*Jesus, thank You for all the amazing treasures You have put in my
life. You are my treasure too! Please help me not to be obsessed
with getting more and more things. Things don't really matter.
Love matters and people matter. Help me to be thankful
and content with the blessings You've given me.*

DON'T WORRY

"Do not worry about tomorrow. Tomorrow will have its own worries.
The troubles we have in a day are enough for one day."

MATTHEW 6:34

It's really easy to get worried about stuff! The first day of school. Losing a tooth. Flying in an airplane for the first time. Taking a test. Getting a shot. A lot of things can freak out a kid! But Jesus tells us not to worry about tomorrow. Did you know that worrying is actually bad for your body? When you worry, it can cause your body to release stress hormones that make your heart work harder, it can cause you to be tired and grumpy, and it can even slow down your body's ability to fight disease. So Jesus tells us simply not to do it! He wants you to have His peace even in the midst of scary situations. If you know something big and kind of scary is coming up tomorrow, trust Jesus to help you through it. Picture yourself carrying everything you are afraid of to Jesus and laying it down before Him. How does it feel to let Jesus have your worries?

---

*Jesus, I know You are strong enough to handle all of my worries.
I bring each of them to You, and I ask You to replace those
worries with the peace that comes from trusting You.*

JUDGING OTHERS

"Do not say what is wrong in other people's lives.
Then other people will not say what is wrong in your life."
MATTHEW 7:1

Have you ever walked into a room and felt like someone was looking at you funny and maybe judging you? Judging is when someone forms an opinion about you quickly without knowing much about you or the situation at all. Being unfairly judged by someone hurts. Everybody seems to be judging everyone and everything these days. There are so many TV shows where judging happens, from how someone sings to how they bake a cake or wear their makeup. Our society is trained to judge people. But to be like Jesus, we need to stop judging other people. We need to love people for who they are—not for what they look like or how well they sing. The next time you meet someone new, be kind. Give them a smile and get to know them for who they are and the gifts God gave them. Look past what they wear and how they look, and see the amazing person God created. Only God can rightly judge people's hearts, motives, and actions. Let God be the judge—and you just be you!

---

*Jesus, forgive me for the times I've judged people
without getting to know who they really are.
Please allow me to see others as You see them.*

ASK, LOOK, AND KNOCK

"Ask, and what you are asking for will be given to you. Look, and what you are looking for you will find. Knock, and the door you are knocking on will be opened to you. Everyone who asks receives what he asks for. Everyone who looks finds what he is looking for. Everyone who knocks has the door opened to him."

MATTHEW 7:7–8

Jesus knows everything about you. Did you know that? Even though He knows exactly what your heart wants and needs, He still wants you to talk to Him about those things. Jesus wants to be your best friend and talk to you about everything. Think about one of your best friends. You like this person because they are fun to be with, they care about you, they share, and you enjoy being with them. You can have that same relationship with Jesus. As you get to know more about Jesus, you'll realize how fun He is to be with. He loves to give you little surprises and blessings. He cares about you more than any other person ever could. The Bible says that He delights in you! He loves being with you and spending special time together. Ask Jesus to become your best friend, and You'll begin to see just how amazing His friendship can be!

Jesus, I really want to get to know You better!
Will You show me how special and fun our friendship can be?

THE GOLDEN RULE

"Do for other people whatever you would like to have them do for you. This is what the Jewish Law and the early preachers said."

MATTHEW 7:12

Jesus taught us about the Golden Rule. This rule has been around since ancient times, and most people, whether they go to church or not, know what it means. The Golden Rule simply means to treat others as you would want them to treat you. This applies to friends, family members— everyone! Think about the last time a friend was upset with you. Were you treating them the way you'd like to be treated? And consider a time when you were upset with a family member. . . . Were they treating you like you like to be treated? It's a good idea to get in the habit of thinking ahead when you are around other people. If you're playing and having a great time but suddenly someone gets upset, stop and think about the Golden Rule. Is everyone treating each other the way they like to be treated? If not, let them know about the Golden Rule and ask Jesus for help putting it into practice.

Jesus, I want to follow the Golden Rule. I want to treat others with kindness and respect, the way I like to be treated and the way You treat me! Please help me to do that when I'm with my friends and family.

THE NARROW DOOR

"Go in through the narrow door. The door is wide and the road is
easy that leads to hell. Many people are going through that door.
But the door is narrow and the road is hard that leads to
life that lasts forever. Few people are finding it."

MATTHEW 7:13–14

As you grow up, you may hear the saying "All roads lead to heaven." But
Jesus tells us that is not true. He says there is a narrow door, and that
door is Him. He is the only way to heaven. A lot of people live to satisfy
their selfish desires. And a lot of good people simply don't know Jesus.
Other people want nothing to do with Jesus because they have had a bad
experience with church or with church people. But that's because they
don't know the real Jesus and how amazing a friendship with Him can
be! Our job is to love Jesus, love others, and be exactly who He created
us to be. When people see that we have a real, everyday friendship with
Jesus, they are going to want to know about it!

---

*Jesus, help me to be the person who shines a bright light
toward the narrow door! I want to show Your love to
others so they can get to know the real You.*

GOOD FRUIT OR BAD FRUIT

"It is true, every good tree has good fruit. Every bad tree
has bad fruit. A good tree cannot have bad fruit.
A bad tree cannot have good fruit."

MATTHEW 7:17–18

Jesus has so much wisdom to share about life. It's all still true today. You've probably watched a movie before where someone seems really nice and lovely on the outside—but on the inside their heart is dark and mean. Think about Rapunzel's mom at the beginning of the movie. She keeps Rapunzel locked in a tower to use her for selfish reasons, pretending to love and care for her. There are people in this world just like that. Jesus had a lot to say about people's hearts. Sometimes it's hard to tell what a person is like by just meeting them. So Jesus wants to give you wisdom and discernment. Discernment is a gift that Jesus gives us to help us know if a person or place is safe or not. Ask Jesus to give you this gift. He will help you to understand if someone is growing good fruit or bad fruit. Bad fruit can spoil anything it touches. When you see bad fruit in a person, talk to Jesus about it and ask Him for wisdom. He will help you know what to do.

---

*Jesus, Your Word tells me that I can ask for wisdom and You'll
give it to me [James 1:5]! I ask that You would help me to
have wisdom and discernment. Help me make right
choices about people and relationships.*

ON THE ROCK

"Whoever hears these words of Mine and does them, will be like
a wise man who built his house on rock. The rain came down.
The water came up. The wind blew and hit the house.
The house did not fall because it was built on rock."

MATTHEW 7:24–25

Have you ever gone to the beach? If so, you've probably seen houses built on the sand. They have structures built underneath them to keep them from falling and collapsing during storms. Still, building a home on the sand is a dangerous risk. Even contractors who build homes on the beach warn that building a home on sand can be a big problem. If a big storm comes, the house can fall apart if it doesn't have a stable foundation. Jesus tells this story in Matthew to teach us about life as a Christian. If we build our lives on the firm foundation of Jesus, when difficult things happen to us, we won't fall apart. We have trust in God! But if we don't have a solid foundation in Jesus, we can fall apart when storms and bad things happen to us. Put your trust in the solid rock of Jesus. He will never let you fall!

---

*Jesus, I am so thankful for my faith. I know You are my strong
foundation that will be with me no matter what
storms and troubles come my way.*

THE AUTHORITY OF JESUS

Then Jesus finished talking. The people were surprised and
wondered about His teaching. He was teaching them as
One Who has the right and the power to teach.
He did not teach as the teachers of the Law.

MATTHEW 7:28–29

You probably know a lot of teachers. You may have teachers at school
and teachers at church, and your parents are your teachers too. But I
bet you know that those teachers can't possibly know everything about
everything. But Jesus does! Imagine being taught by someone who
created all things and really does know the answer to everything! The
amazing news is that Jesus wants to teach you Himself. Isaiah 54:13 says,
"All your children will be taught by the LORD, and great will be their
peace" (NIV). If you've accepted Jesus as Your Savior, His Spirit is alive
in you, teaching you all things. Jesus has complete authority and power
over all things. Why is this important for you? It means that you can
go to Jesus with all your questions. It means that He has authority over
everything that might come your way. It means that He is bigger than all
of your problems, failures, and fears. And you have access to this power
at every moment!

---

*I'm so thankful that You have authority over my life, Jesus!
I ask You to teach me and lead me as I live this life You've given me.*

COMPASSION

A man with a bad skin disease came and got down before [Jesus]
and worshiped Him. He said, "Lord, if You will, You can heal
me!" Then Jesus put His hand on him and said, "I will.
You are healed!" At once the man was healed.

MATTHEW 8:2–3

Back in Bible times leprosy was a scary disease with no cure. If people
got sick with leprosy, they were banished from their homes and sent to
live with other sick people called "lepers." Some forms of leprosy were
contagious, so of course no one would want to touch someone with this
disease. But Jesus did! He had compassion on this man and reached out
His hands to him. Jesus touched the leper and healed him.

How can you have more compassion for people? Maybe Jesus will
call you to become a nurse or a doctor in the medical field. Maybe you
have compassion for sick animals and could become a veterinarian.
There are lots of ways to develop and practice compassion for others.
Maybe the next time a family member is sick you could offer to help
them in some way. Ask Jesus for more opportunities to show compassion.
Compassionate people show the love of Jesus to a hurting world.

---

*Jesus, please help me to see people who are in need
and give me wisdom to know how to help them.
I want to be a compassionate person.*

THE WIND AND
WAVES OBEY JESUS

At once a bad storm came over the lake. The waves were covering
the boat. Jesus was sleeping. His followers went to Him and called,
"Help us, Lord, or we will die!" He said to them, "Why are you
afraid? You have so little faith!" Then He stood up. He spoke
sharp words to the wind and the waves. Then the wind
stopped blowing. Then men were surprised and wondered
about it. They said, "What kind of a man is He?
Even the winds and the waves obey Him."
MATTHEW 8:24–27

Have you ever been outside when a storm came on suddenly? It can
be a very scary experience! Wind and lightning can do great damage.
Even though the disciples were experienced fishermen and knew their
way around boats and storms, this storm that started had them worried.
The waves were sweeping up over the boat, and the disciples thought
they were going to drown! They woke Jesus, begging for help. He spoke
to the wind and waves and told them to stop. And they did! Isn't that
amazing? Jesus still holds the same power over all of nature today. You
can always ask Him for help.

---

*Lord, I'm amazed at Your power. All of nature responds to Your
commands. Please give me the faith to believe in Your power.*

CHANGE YOUR THOUGHTS

Jesus knew what they were thinking. He said,
"Why do you think bad thoughts in your hearts?"
MATTHEW 9:4

Some teachers of the law were judging Jesus. Jesus knew what they were thinking and called them out on it. Another translation says, "Why do you entertain evil thoughts in your hearts?" (NIV). We can choose what we think about. When you "entertain a thought," you think about it a lot and won't stop yourself from thinking about it. Finally, you allow it to take root in your heart, which can affect your behavior. Another scripture tells us what to do about these wrong thoughts that try to take root in us: "We break down every thought and proud thing that puts itself up against the wisdom of God. We take hold of every thought and make it obey Christ" (2 Corinthians 10:5). To be like Jesus, we want to entertain only thoughts that are for God and of God. How do we "break down" wrong thoughts and make them obey Christ? When you have a bad or scary thought, take it directly to Jesus. Ask Him to take the thought away. Then focus on something good. Ask Jesus to fill your mind with something that comes from Him.

Jesus, please help me to entertain good thoughts that will make You happy. Remind me that I have a choice in what I think about and that You can help me change my thoughts.

FRIEND OF SINNERS

Jesus heard [the religious law-keepers] and said, "People who are well do not need a doctor. But go and understand these words, 'I want loving-kindness and not a gift to be given.' For I have not come to call good people. I have come to call those who are sinners."

MATTHEW 9:12–13

Jesus went to visit a man named Matthew, a tax collector. He was hated by the Jewish people because tax collectors back then were known for cheating people. Jesus had dinner with Matthew and some of Matthew's tax collector friends. The Pharisees asked the disciples why their teacher would do such a terrible thing as eat with tax collectors and sinners. Jesus wisely responded that it's sick people who need a doctor, not healthy people. Jesus was a friend of sinners and a doctor to the sick. That means that He had the healing and the answers that sinful people needed to change their lives. Jesus asked Matthew to follow Him, so Matthew left his job and his sinning, and did what Jesus asked. Jesus had the answers Matthew needed. He has the answers for our sinful world too. Pray for the people around you who need Jesus, and ask for opportunities to share God's love with them.

Jesus, please fill me with loving-kindness for the people around me. Even the ones who are hard to love. Help me be a friend to all those who need You.

JESUS HEALS A YOUNG GIRL

While Jesus talked to [His disciples], a leader of the people
came and got down before Him, and worshiped Him.
He said, "My daughter has just died. But come,
lay Your hand on her and she will live."
MATTHEW 9:18

Jesus went to the home of a young girl who had just died. A crowd was mourning her death outside. They did not believe that Jesus could bring the dead to life. They even laughed at Jesus when He came to the house. But the girl's father did believe. Jesus took the girl by her hand, and she got up! To the crowd, this situation seemed hopeless. The girl was dead. What could anyone do? But the father trusted that Jesus was who He said He was. He went to Jesus and asked for help, and Jesus answered. Ask Jesus to take your hand like He took this little girl's hand. Jesus loves children, and you are very important to Him! Your faith in the God of miracles will make all the difference in your life. Jesus is with you. He takes hold of your hand.

---

*Jesus, please take hold of my hand and walk with me every
day of my life on this earth. I'm so thankful for Your love.
I trust You to do the impossible. I love You, Jesus!*

SIMPLE FAITH

Then Jesus turned around. He saw [the bleeding woman]
and said, "Daughter, take hope! Your faith has healed
you." At once the woman was healed.

MATTHEW 9:22

A woman with a bleeding disorder secretly came to Jesus. She didn't want attention. The Bible tells us she had this disease for twelve years. She was labeled as "unclean" and was considered untouchable. She thought to herself that if she could just touch the tassels on the hem of Jesus' tunic, she would be healed. She reached out for Jesus and touched the hem of His garment and was healed instantly. She tried to slip away unnoticed, but Jesus felt power go out from Him and called to her. He wanted her to know that it was her faith in God that healed her. And maybe He wanted the crowd to know that regardless of how a person has been labeled, they are still worthy of love and respect. In any case, this woman showed simple faith in a miraculous God, and she was healed. If you've just started a friendship with Jesus, your faith will continue to grow each day as you put your trust in Him. He will show you that even if your faith is small and new, He is a miraculous God who can be trusted.

Jesus, thank You for showing me who You are. I trust that You are
a God of miracles and that my simple faith in You is enough.

MORE FAITH

Then Jesus put His hands on [the blind men's] eyes and said,
"You will have what you want because you have faith."

MATTHEW 9:29

After Jesus healed the little girl, He left her house and two blind men
followed Him. They asked Jesus to have mercy on them. They called
Jesus the "Son of David" because the Old Testament said that Jesus the
Messiah would be a descendant of King David. The Old Testament also
said that the Messiah would give sight to the blind. Even though these
guys were blind, they probably knew what the Old Testament said about
the Messiah by hearing it from others. Jesus didn't heal these blind men
immediately. First He asked them if they believed that Jesus would be
able to heal them. He wanted to know about their faith. After they told
Jesus that they did believe in Him, He healed them. What's in our hearts
is very important to Jesus. What's in your heart today? Do you know that
Jesus loves you? Do you have faith that He can do anything? If there is
something you're not sure that God can do, bring that to Jesus and ask
Him for help to believe.

*Jesus, please fill me with more and more faith as I learn
to trust in You. Like these blind men, I want to
believe that You can do anything!*

SHEEP WITHOUT A SHEPHERD

As [Jesus] saw many people, He had loving-pity on them.
They were troubled and were walking around everywhere.
They were like sheep without a shepherd.

MATTHEW 9:36

Sheep are born with an instinct to follow the leader. They will usually follow whatever the sheep in front of them are doing—even if it is dangerous or stupid. I've heard it said that if one sheep jumps over a cliff, the rest of them will do it too. When Jesus came to earth, He saw that the people were acting like sheep without a shepherd. Most people were making bad choices and following those around them who were also making bad choices. Some people look at people making bad decisions and have no compassion for them. They judge them harshly and leave them to their consequences. But not Jesus. The Bible says that He had compassion on these people. He knew what caused them to make poor choices. He loved them and wanted to help. He came to be the Good Shepherd, to lead people to Himself. Jesus demonstrated servant leadership by setting an example of loving others and serving their needs. He taught that we must treat each other with kindness and respect. Are you a leader or a follower? Ask Jesus to help You lead others well while You follow Him.

Jesus, thank You for leading me. Help me to be the kind
of leader that has compassion and love for others.

THE FRIENDS OF JESUS

Jesus called His twelve followers to Him. He gave them power to put out demons and to heal all kinds of sickness and disease.

MATTHEW 10:1

Jesus called His disciples to follow Him. He wasn't mean and bossy, demanding that these twelve guys do exactly what He said. He asked them to follow Him, and He gave them each a choice. They became His friends. He chose normal, everyday guys. Guys who probably thought they could never be used by God. I mean, He chose fishermen, and one of His followers was even a former sinful tax collector! He gave these regular guys extraordinary power to change the world. Through Jesus' power, they were able to heal sickness and cast out demons. Jesus used these disciples to show that God can use anyone. The same is true today. You may not think that you have any great talents or gifts that God can use. But God can use anything you bring to Him and turn it into something that brings honor to Him and blessing to You. If you are a friend of Jesus, He has great plans for you! Check out what God's Word has to say about that: " 'For I know the plans I have for you,' declares the LORD, 'plans to prosper you and not to harm you, plans to give you hope and a future' " (Jeremiah 29:11 NIV).

Jesus, I trust Your great plans for me. I bring all that I have to You to use. Thanks for being my friend.

GIVE MUCH

"You have received much, now give much."
MATTHEW 10:8

Matthew 10:8 has been quoted many ways in many places, but the basic idea is that if you have been given much, much is expected. That means that you can't keep your gifts, talents, and blessings to yourself. Dr. Ben Carson said, "Happiness doesn't result from what we get, but from what we give." You will never be a happy person if you keep everything to yourself. You may not have a lot of money, but you do have something that you can always give away—love. You've been given tons of love! To be like Jesus, we must love the people around us by using what we've been given. This doesn't mean just things, although sometimes it's definitely important to share our things. It also means the gifts and qualities that God has given us. Maybe you're a great reader. Can you help someone else who is just learning to read? Can you read to an elderly person who has lost her eyesight? Maybe you've been blessed with a great singing voice. Can you help sing your baby sister to sleep? Can you sing in church as you help other people worship God? Ask God to show you how you can use your gifts and blessings to serve other people.

Jesus, thank You for the gifts and blessings You've given me. Open my eyes to see the needs of others, and help me use my gifts to meet those needs.

THE WORDS OF GOD

"When you are put into their hands, do not worry what you will say
or how you will say it. The words will be given you when the
time comes. It will not be you who will speak the words.
The Spirit of your Father will speak through you."

MATTHEW 10:19–20

Sometimes in your life, you'll be asked to speak up about your faith in
God. This might happen at school or on your neighborhood playground.
Maybe at gymnastics class or karate. As a follower of Jesus, you're called
to share your faith with others. Maybe you see something bad happening
or you find a kid sitting all alone and scared about something. You may
get a sense in your heart that you're supposed to do or say something
to help! But this is not something to worry about. Want to know why?
Because in Matthew 10:19–20, Jesus said that the words we're supposed
to say will be given to us. If you ask Jesus for help, He'll give you the
perfect thing to say or do at just the right time. And even if you feel
like you've messed it up or said the wrong thing, don't worry about that
either! Jesus can take what you've said or done and turn it into something
good.

---

*Jesus, thank You for preparing me and teaching me about
everything! I'm so thankful I don't have to worry about
any situation because You are always with me!*

MORE IMPORTANT

"Are not two small birds sold for a very small piece of money?
And yet not one of the birds falls to the earth without your
Father knowing it. God knows how many hairs you
have on your head. So do not be afraid. You are
more important than many small birds."

MATTHEW 10:29–31

Have you ever felt like you don't really matter, or that nobody is listening to your thoughts and feelings? If you have brothers and sisters, you've probably felt ignored by them before. Check out what the psalmist said in Psalm 139: "For you [God] created my inmost being; you knit me together in my mother's womb. I praise you because I am fearfully and wonderfully made; your works are wonderful, I know that full well" (verses 13–14 NIV). Can you imagine that? It's all true. Imagine Jesus putting you together as you were growing in your mom's tummy. He knows everything about you, and He cares for you more than anything else in creation. You are so important to Him that He died for you on the cross so that you could be with Him forever. The next time you're feeling down or unimportant, remember who made you and how much He loves you!

Jesus, I bring my sadness to You and ask You to fill me up with Your truth. You made me, and I'm important—simply because You said so!

A CUP OF WATER

"For sure, I tell you, anyone who gives a cup of cold water to one of these little ones because he follows Me, will not lose his reward."

MATTHEW 10:42

You don't have to have a lot to give to others in order to serve them. Here are some great quotes about serving others from famous people:

- *"Those who are the happiest are those who do the most for others."* —Booker T. Washington

- *"Love is the ultimate gift of ourselves to others. When we stop giving we stop loving, when we stop loving we stop growing, and unless we grow we will never attain personal fulfillment. . . . It is through love we encounter God."* —Mother Teresa

- *"You have not lived today until you have done something for someone who can never repay you."* —John Bunyan

- *"Be devoted to one another in love. Honor one another above yourselves."* —Romans 12:10 NIV

Have you ever done something for someone else just because you love them and not expecting anything in return? To be like Jesus, serving others needs to be something we do every day. Ask Jesus to give you eyes to see the needs of others, and then do what you can with what you have. Even if it's simply giving a cup of water to someone who is thirsty.

Jesus, help me serve others like You do.

COME TO JESUS

"Come to Me, all of you who work and have heavy loads. I will give you rest. Follow My teachings and learn from Me. I am gentle and do not have pride. You will have rest for your souls. For My way of carrying a load is easy and My load is not heavy."

MATTHEW 11:28–30

Jesus says, "Come to me." He calls us to bring all of our burdens and lay them at His feet. He wants to take away the heavy load we're carrying in our hearts, which He likened to the weight of a yoke that oxen wear for the purpose of dragging something or carrying heavy equipment. Jesus liked to use visual imagery to get His meaning across. Can't you just picture all the burdens you are carrying right now strapped to your back like a yoke on a pair of oxen plowing a field? Now imagine yourself unloading each burden onto Jesus' shoulders instead.

Jesus tells us many times throughout the Gospels not to worry. Worrying about something will never help you. Worry makes things worse and makes burdens seem larger. Jesus wants us to find rest in Him. Hear His gentle words rush over you: "Come to Me," and you'll find rest for your soul.

Jesus, thank You for taking my burdens. I give them fully to You. Help me not to take them back! I want the rest and peace that You are offering.

A DIFFERENT KIND OF LEADER

"See! My Servant Whom I have chosen! My much Loved, in Whom
My soul is well pleased! I will put My Spirit in Him. He will say to
the nations what is right from wrong. He will not fight or speak
with a loud voice. No man will hear His voice in the streets. He will
not break a broken branch. He will not put out a little fire until He
makes things right. In His name the nations will have hope."

MATTHEW 12:18–21

The famous African American civil rights leader Martin Luther King
Jr. said that "everybody can be great, because everybody can serve." Jesus
was all about servant leadership. That means He led His followers by
showing them how to love and serve other people. He didn't arrive as a
king who would sit on His throne and be served. He came to serve and
show love. He even washed His disciples' dusty feet to make His point
very clear. He loved them. And loving leaders serve their people. The
people in Bible times were expecting their Messiah to come with victory
and rule over the wicked. They weren't sure what to do with Jesus because
He came as a gentle servant, quietly showing the way to lead others to
truth and freedom. What kind of leader are you? Ask Jesus to help you
lead like He does!

Jesus, show me how to lead others out of love.
Let me point the way to hope in You.

MORE ABOUT WORDS

"A good man will speak good things because of the good in him.
A bad man will speak bad things because of the sin in him."
MATTHEW 12:35

You've probably heard the saying "If you can't say something nice, don't say anything at all." Jesus always spoke the truth, and He did it in a firm but loving way. You can ask Jesus for help to do the same thing. Sometimes you might be tempted to brag to others about something you've done well or something you have that others don't. For instance, it might be true that you get to go to Disney World and someone else doesn't, but you can share that information in a loving way or simply choose not to share about your trip at all if it would make your listeners feel sad that they don't get to go on a nice vacation.

Asking Jesus for wisdom with your words is really important. You can always apologize if you say the wrong thing, but you can't ever take those words back once they're out of your mouth. The book of James gives us some really good advice about this: "My dear brothers and sisters, take note of this: Everyone should be quick to listen, slow to speak and slow to become angry" (James 1:19 NIV).

Jesus, please help me to be quick to listen and slow to speak.
Give me wisdom as I choose my words.

THE FAMILY OF GOD

*"Whoever does what My father in heaven wants him to
do is My brother and My sister and My mother."*

MATTHEW 12:50

Family is important to Jesus. Psalm 68:6 tells us that "God sets the lonely in families" (NIV). He made us to be in a community with other people. We learn from each other and grow and share God's love when we live in relationships with other people. God doesn't want us to be lonely. You are a child of God, so that means you are part of God's family! That also means that other Christians all over the world are your brothers and sisters in Christ. Being part of the family of God means that you share with your fellow believers and you can encourage one another. If you are having a hard time finding good friends right now, ask Jesus for help! He cares about your relationships and wants you to have the family of God around you to help you in this life. If you are feeling lonely, tell Jesus about it! He hears your prayers and promises to help you.

---

*Jesus, sometimes I feel alone, and I need help with my
friendships. Will You help me find other believers who love
You and want to follow You? Please show me what
it means to be a part of Your family.*

PICTURE STORIES

"This is why I speak to [the crowds] in picture-stories.
They have eyes but they do not see. They have ears but
they do not hear and they do not understand."

MATTHEW 13:13

Jesus was an amazing storyteller! People loved to listen to Him tell stories.
The great thing is that all His stories have deeper meaning. He told people
"parables," which is another name for picture stories. He wanted people
to use their imagination and understand the deeper meanings of His
stories. He told stories about grapevines and vineyards to show how we,
the branches, must stay attached to Jesus, the Vine, if we want to grow
in faith. He told stories about farmers and seeds to encourage leaders to
continue sharing the good news of Jesus. He told stories about a woman
baking bread, a man searching for treasure, and a shopkeeper looking
for pearls. Many of the people listening were enemies of Jesus, and they
didn't understand what His picture stories meant. But the people who
loved God understood and were encouraged by the stories. Ask Jesus to
give you eyes that see and ears that hear so that you can understand what
Jesus is saying to you too.

---

*Jesus, I love to hear Your stories. As I read them in the Bible,
please give me eyes to see and ears to hear
what You want me to know.*

SMALL BEGINNINGS

Jesus told [the crowd] another picture-story. He said, "The holy
nation of heaven is like mustard seed which a man planted in his
field. It is the smallest of seeds. But when it is full-grown, it is larger
than the grain of the fields and it becomes a tree. The birds
of the sky come and stay in its branches."

MATTHEW 13:31–32

Have you ever seen a mustard seed? Your mom might have some in her
spice rack. Ask her to show them to you, or take a look at them the
next time you're at the grocery store. They were considered the smallest
of garden seeds that people would plant, and yet they would grow into
trees large enough for birds to build nests in them. Jesus said that the
kingdom of God is like the mustard seed. It started small with Jesus
and His twelve disciples. Those disciples shared about Jesus and brought
more people to know Him. This continued down through the ages, and
here we are today where you are learning about Jesus too! When you tell
someone else about faith in Jesus, you are adding to God's kingdom as
well. Isn't that amazing? The kingdom of God had very small beginnings,
but as you can see, it grew into a worldwide movement. You might be
small now, but as you grow you will see that God has great things in store
for you your whole life!

---

*Jesus, thank You for my small beginnings. As I continue to
follow You, I know You have great plans for my life.*

TRUST HIM

*[Jesus] did not do many powerful works [in His hometown]
because they did not put their trust in Him.*
MATTHEW 13:58

As Jesus was traveling and sharing about the kingdom of God, He came back to His hometown. He began to share the Good News like He'd done everywhere else. At first the people were amazed. But then they got upset and offended. They wondered who this guy thought He was. They had known Him since He was a little boy! How could He say He was the Son of God? These people didn't believe what Jesus was saying was true because they couldn't look past the person to hear the truth from God. Jesus didn't do many miracles in His hometown because the people didn't have any faith. This verse tells us what happens when we don't trust Jesus. If we're believing that Jesus is who He says He is, then we'll accept the miracles He wants to do in our lives. If we have a hard time trusting Jesus, we won't be able to see the miracles all around us. Take a minute and think about your life. What miracles have you already experienced? Ask Jesus to help you see them. Talk about them with your family.

---

*Jesus, thank You for doing miracles in my life.
Please give me eyes to see the ways You bless me every day.*

FIVE LOAVES AND TWO FISH

[Jesus] told the people to sit down on the grass. Then He took
the five loaves of bread and two fish. He looked up to heaven and
gave thanks. He broke the loaves in pieces and gave them to
His followers. The followers gave them to the people.

MATTHEW 14:19

The story of the loaves and fishes is an amazing miracle. A large
crowd was following Jesus, so He stopped and healed their sick. He
showed the crowd compassion. It was getting late, and Jesus' disciples
encouraged Him to send the crowd away so they could get some food.
But Jesus wanted to continue ministering to the crowd, so instead of
sending them away, He asked them all to sit down on the grass. All
they had available to them was five loaves of bread and two fish. Jesus
took what they had and gave thanks for it. The food multiplied in Jesus'
hands, and His disciples started passing out all the food. There was so
much left over that they had twelve basketsful left over! Did you know
that more than five thousand people were fed by those five loaves of
bread and two fish? Jesus used what He had and made a miracle out of
it. Will you allow Jesus to use what you have?

---

*Jesus, I offer You everything I have—my gifts and talents and
blessings. Please use me as You grow Your kingdom.*

STEP OUT OF THE BOAT

Jesus said, "Come!" Peter got out of the boat
and walked on the water to Jesus.
MATTHEW 14:29

When our eyes are focused on Jesus, He gives us the ability to rise above the storms of life. But just like Peter, when we get distracted and scared by the waves and problems all around us, we start to sink. Peter cried out to God for help when he realized how crazy and unbelievable it seemed to step out in faith! But the Bible says that "immediately Jesus reached out his hand and caught him" (Matthew 14:31 NIV). Are you having trouble stepping out in faith and keeping your eyes on Jesus? Do you keep looking at your problems instead of looking for God? Ask God to reach out His hand to you just like He did with Peter. Ask Him to forgive you for doubting and to give you supernatural power to keep your eyes focused on Him. Trust Him to give you strength and peace in all situations.

---

*Jesus, sometimes I'm scared to step out in faith and do the things
You ask me to. I forget to keep my eyes on You, and I look at everyone
and everything else instead. Please fill me with Your power to
overcome so that I can keep focused on You!*

FAR FROM GOD

"These people show respect to Me with their mouth, but their
heart is far from Me. Their worship of Me is worth nothing.
They teach what men have made up."

MATTHEW 15:8–9

Do you happen to know anyone who says they love God but never acts
like it? Or maybe you have a friend who comes to your church but acts
mean at school. You've probably hear the saying "Actions speak louder
than words." People can say a lot of things, but it's what's inside their
hearts that really matters. The Pharisees in Jesus' day knew a lot about
God and all the Old Testament laws. In fact, they prided themselves
on looking good on the outside and following all the laws strictly. They
thought they knew everything about God, but they were actually very
far from Him. Following Jesus doesn't mean following all the rules and
never messing up. Following Jesus means you have a real friendship with
Him in which you learn His Word and talk to Him about it. You get to
know His heart and His love for you. You love Him back, and you share
that love with others.

---

*Jesus, I want to know the real You. Bless our friendship
and remind me that You want to have conversations
with me all day long. Be close to my heart, Jesus.*

CHURCH ON THE ROCK

"On this rock I will build My church. The powers of hell
will not be able to have power over My church."

MATTHEW 16:18

Jesus was talking to Simon Peter and asking Him who Simon Peter thought Jesus was. Simon Peter told Jesus that he believed Jesus was the Christ, the Son of the living God. Jesus blessed Simon Peter, shortened his name to Peter, and declared that He would build His church on the rock. Peter became a great leader in the church and wrote this: "The Lord Jesus is the 'stone' that lives. The people of the world did not want this stone. But he was the stone God chose. To God he was worth much. So come to him. You also are like living stones. Let yourselves be used to build a spiritual temple—to be holy priests who offer spiritual sacrifices to God. He will accept those sacrifices through Jesus Christ" (1 Peter 2:4–5 ICB). The Bible tells us that if we follow Jesus, we are part of His church. We are rocks that build up the church with Jesus as our secure foundation. Will you allow Jesus to help build His church through you?

---

*Jesus, I'm so thankful to be a part of Your kingdom.
I'm happy that You want to build Your church through me.*

FOLLOWING JESUS

Jesus said to His followers, "If anyone wants to be My follower,
he must forget about himself. He must take up
his cross and follow Me."

MATTHEW 16:24

A true follower of Jesus is not a selfish person. Jesus tells us that to be His follower, we need to forget about ourselves and our needs. He means that we need to trust God to take care of us instead of being worried about the stuff we think we need. Back in Bible times, following Jesus was a dangerous thing to do. Many of His followers were killed because of their faith. Thankfully, we don't live in a country where we are persecuted to death for believing in Jesus. But Jesus still calls us to the same kind of faith. The kind of faith where you trust Jesus for everything—your food, your safety, your very life. The disciples risked everything to follow Jesus, and the kingdom of God has spread to all the nations because of it. What is Jesus asking you to do to help grow His kingdom? Take courage from the disciples who died for their faith! If they can trust Jesus with their lives, can you trust Jesus to help you share His love with a friend in need?

---

*Jesus, please give me the courage to help grow Your kingdom by
sharing my faith with others. I trust You to take care of me!*

UNAFRAID

When the followers heard [God speaking], they got down on the ground on their faces and were very much afraid. Jesus came and put His hand on them. He said, "Get up! Do not be afraid."
MATTHEW 17:6-7

Jesus allowed some of His followers to go with Him on a mountain where a miracle took place. Jesus' face began to shine like the sun, and His clothes turned white like the light. Moses and Elijah appeared to them, and then they heard God's voice. The disciples were terrified. Jesus knew they were scared, so He went over to them and touched them. He told them they had nothing to be afraid of. Jesus is so caring! When you're with Him, you have no reason to be afraid. You can trust Him completely because everything He does, He does out of love for you. He never lies, and He always keeps His promises. He can turn any bad situation around and use it for good. Remember Romans 8:28 says, "We know that in everything God works for the good of those who love him" (ICB). That's why you don't have to be afraid when things become a little scary. Jesus is with you, and you can trust Him to care lovingly for you.

Thank You that I never have to be afraid, Jesus. I know Your plans for my life are good and that I can trust You.

MUSTARD-SEED FAITH

"For sure, I tell you, if you have faith as a mustard seed,
you will say to this mountain, 'Move from here to over there,'
and it would move over. You will be able to do anything."

MATTHEW 17:20

Remember that mustard seed we talked about before? Remember how tiny it is? The disciples were having a hard time getting a job done. They weren't so sure about this new power that Jesus had given them. Jesus reminded them that it was the power of God working inside them, not their own power, that gave them the ability to get the job done. The same is true for us. When we have small faith in a huge God, anything is possible. Hudson Taylor was a missionary to China for over fifty years. He depended on God to meet his needs in a dangerous foreign country when he ran out of money. Taylor said, "You do not need a great faith, but faith in a great God." Hudson Taylor believed in mustard-seed faith, and Jesus is calling us to have that kind of faith too. Our part is trusting that Jesus is all powerful and can do anything. God's part is to be exactly who He is: all powerful and faithful.

*Jesus, I trust You to be faithful and all-powerful in my life.
Though my faith is small, I know that Your power is big!*

CHILDREN AND JESUS

Jesus took a little child and put him among them. He said,
"For sure, I tell you, unless you have a change of heart and become
like a little child, you will not get into the holy nation of heaven.
Whoever is without pride as this little child is the greatest
in the holy nation of heaven. Whoever receives a
little child because of Me receives Me."

MATTHEW 18:2–5

Jesus loves kids! All through the Bible we see Jesus caring for children and loving them. Author and speaker Beth Moore said as a child she loved the picture of Jesus with children climbing on His lap. And because of the big smile on Jesus' face in that work of art, she thought that children must make Jesus very happy. As a child, Beth Moore knew that Jesus loved children. Other pictures of Jesus with adults never showed Jesus as happy as He was when He was with kids. Children are so important to Jesus because they have a lot to teach the world. That's right! The way you think and believe is the way Jesus wants grown-ups to believe too. He wants us to have simple, childlike faith.

Jesus, I'm so thankful that You think I'm important.
That's pretty amazing! Help me share my faith with
everyone, especially the adults in my life.

JESUS PROTECTS YOU

"Be sure you do not hate one of these little children. I tell you,
they have angels who are always looking into the
face of My Father in heaven."

MATTHEW 18:10

The Bible tells us that children have angels watching out for them who report straight to God. Doesn't that make you feel loved and safe? When I was a little girl, I was lost at an amusement park. I saw the haunted house and walked through it all by myself. I was way too young to be away from my family. Of course the haunted house was scary, and I was all alone. At one point, I looked up, and a tall, bright-looking man took my hand and led me to the exit where I soon found my family. The man disappeared after that. Was he an angel? I won't know for sure until I get to heaven, but I like to believe he was. Angels aren't beings to worship; they are God's messengers and warriors. God has very special plans for your life, and He sends His angels to guard and protect you so that those plans happen. To be more like Jesus, it's helpful to know more about His character. Know that He loves and protects you always.

---

*Jesus, thank You for sending Your angels to guard and protect me!
I feel safe knowing that You love me in this way.*

NO ONE LEFT BEHIND

"A man has one hundred sheep and one of them is lost. Will he not leave the ninety-nine and go to the mountains to look for that one lost sheep? If he finds it, for sure, I tell you, he will have more joy over that one, than over the ninety-nine that were not lost. I tell you, My Father in heaven does not want one of these little children to be lost."

MATTHEW 18:12–14

Jesus doesn't want anyone to be left behind. Each child of His is precious and important. Jesus tells another picture story to illustrate this fact. Shepherds don't want to lose any of their sheep. If they know that even one of them has wandered off, they'll go searching for it. Second Peter 3:9 says, "The Lord isn't really being slow about his promise, as some people think. No, he is being patient for your sake. He does not want anyone to be destroyed, but wants everyone to repent" (NLT). Sometimes it takes awhile for someone to come to know Jesus, even if they've been hearing about Him for a long time. Jesus is patient with us. He wants all of us to know His love and goodness. Be patient with your friends and family who don't love Jesus. Pray for them and know that Jesus is waiting patiently for them too.

---

*Jesus, help me be patient and pray for my family
and friends who need Your love.*

PRAYING TOGETHER

"Where two or three are gathered together
in My name, there I am with them."
MATTHEW 18:20

Do you pray with Mom and Dad before bed? Jesus says something powerful happens when believers pray together. Sometimes it might feel weird to pray out loud in front of other people, but your prayers together are powerful. Pastor and author Max Lucado said that because of the power of God, our prayers make a difference—even if it seems awkward or difficult for us. *The Message* says it this way: "Take this most seriously: A yes on earth is yes in heaven; a no on earth is no in heaven. What you say to one another is eternal. I mean this. When two of you get together on anything at all on earth and make a prayer of it, my Father in heaven goes into action. And when two or three of you are together because of me, you can be sure that I'll be there" (Matthew 18:18–20). When we ask Jesus for His plans and ideas to happen alongside other people who also have the Holy Spirit living inside of them, amazing things happen. Tonight at bedtime, take turns talking to God with your parents or family members. Ask for His will to be done in a specific situation that effects your family.

Jesus, thank You for being with us in
powerful ways when we pray together.

FORGIVING OTHERS

"So will My Father in heaven do to you, if each one of you
does not forgive his brother from his heart."

MATTHEW 18:35

Jesus told His disciples another picture story about a man who owed His master a lot of money. He didn't have it to pay back when the time came, so he begged the master to let him go. The master forgave his debts and let him go. But that same man went to his fellow servant and demanded that he pay him back some money he owed him. Instead of letting him go like the master had done with him, he sent him to prison. The other servants told on this guy, and the master was very angry and sent him to prison for his poor choice. The master forgave his debt, so the man should have done the same for someone else. Jesus told this story to help us remember that God has forgiven all of our sins, so we need to forgive other people when they hurt us or do something wrong against us. To forgive means that we let go of our right to punish someone for what they've done wrong. We won't hold it against them, and we'll leave the consequences up to God. Do you have anyone in your life whom you need to forgive? Ask Jesus to help you do it.

---

*Jesus, help me to forgive _____ (my friend, my brother
or sister, etc.). I release them into Your hands.
Please help me to love them with Your love.*

YOU MATTER TO JESUS

Jesus said, "Let the little children come to Me. Do not stop them.
The holy nation of heaven is made up of ones like these."

MATTHEW 19:14

Have you ever heard the song "Jesus Loves the Little Children"? If not, ask a grown-up to sing it for you. The song reminds us how precious children are to Jesus. The Bible calls children a gift and a blessing. God's Word also has a message specifically for young people like yourself: "Don't let anyone look down on you because you are young, but set an example for the believers in speech, in conduct, in love, in faith and in purity" (1 Timothy 4:12 NIV). Whenever you feel invisible or unwanted in a situation, remember what Jesus says about you! You are loved. You are a blessing. You are a gift! So don't let people look down on you. You are valued by God, and your opinions and thoughts matter. How do you do this? You set an example. You do the right thing because You love God. People will see that and take notice. No matter what anyone else thinks of you, you matter to Jesus!

Jesus, I'm kind of amazed that my thoughts and opinions matter to You! I'm just a kid! Thanks for treating me with love and respect. Help me to be a good example of Your love to others.

GOD'S POWER, NOT MINE

Jesus looked at [his disciples] and said, "This cannot be
done by men. But with God all things can be done."
MATTHEW 19:26

Remember awhile back when we talked about the disciples having a
hard time carrying out God's plan? They were trying to do it in their
own strength. Jesus reminded them that it wasn't their own power they
needed to have faith in, but God's! *The Message* says it this way: "No
chance at all if you think you can pull it off yourself. Every chance in the
world if you trust God to do it." This should greatly encourage you to put
your faith in God's power. Even if you're small and not very strong yet,
God is bigger. Even if you can't seem to figure out what gifts God might
have given you, He is at work in you. It's true, you have no chance at all
if you think you can do everything in your own power. You will get tired,
give up, fail. But you have every chance in the world if you trust Jesus!
The next time you're facing something big, remember that Jesus' power
is at work in you. As Philippians 4:13 says, "I can do everything through
Christ, who gives me strength" (NLT).

Jesus, I trust that with Your power, everything is possible.
Thank You for working in me!

ME FIRST!

"Many who are first will be last. Many who are last will be first."
MATTHEW 19:30

It's fun to be first in line for things. Do you have line leaders at your school? You might feel just a little more important when you get to line up first and everyone else follows you. There's nothing wrong with being the leader and getting excited that everyone in class gets to follow you. The problems come when you want to be first at everything, all the time. Many grown-ups have never outgrown the "me first" mentality. These people end up having broken relationships with God and people. Jesus shows us another way. Jesus put other people first, and He served them. Jesus tells us that in the kingdom of heaven, the first will be last and the last will be first. Jesus also tells us that it doesn't matter if you are rich or poor, important in today's society or hated by the world, famous or unknown—those things don't get you into heaven any faster. In God's kingdom, we belong simply because of Jesus' love for us!

Jesus, forgive me when I get selfish and want to be first at everything. Help me to have love for others and to put them first. Thank You that I belong simply because You love me.

A SERVANT KING

"Whoever wants to be great among you, let him care for you.
Whoever wants to be first among you, let him be your servant.
For the Son of Man came not to be cared for. He came to care for
others. He came to give His life so that many could be bought
by His blood and made free from the punishment of sin."

MATTHEW 20:26–28

Jesus' ways were so different from other kings. Rightfully, He was creator
and leader of the whole world. Yet He came to be a servant. The famous
theologian Augustine asked and answered this question: "What does
love look like? It has the hands to help others. It has the feet to hasten
to the poor and needy. It has eyes to see misery and want. It has the ears
to hear the sighs and sorrows of men. That is what love looks like." Love
looks like Jesus. Love looks like serving others. Jesus came to show a
better way to the world. The way of love. What does love look like to
you? Can you think of several people who show love well? Why do you
consider them to be loving?

---

*Jesus, thank You for the loving people I have in my life. They show
their love by serving others. Help me to show love in this way too.*

SHOUT FOR JESUS

[The religious leaders] heard the children calling in the house of
God and saying, "Greatest One! Son of David!" The leaders were
very angry. They said to Jesus, "Do you hear what these children
are saying?" Jesus said to them, "Yes, have you not read the
writings, 'Even little children and babies will honor Him'?"

MATTHEW 21:15–16

When the Pharisees heard the children shouting praises to Jesus, they
were upset and offended. Jesus quoted a psalm in the Old Testament to
the Pharisees that says, "You have taught children and infants to tell of
your strength, silencing your enemies and all who oppose you" (Psalm
8:2 NLT). Do you like to sing at church? Do you have a favorite worship
song? Singing is one of the ways we can worship Jesus. Your praises make
Jesus happy. He loves to hear His children praise Him. Praising Jesus is a
very powerful thing. The Bible says it can even silence our enemies. The
next time you are tempted to complain about something, try praising
Jesus instead. Thank Him for who He is and what He has done for you.
Sing to Him. You'll be amazed at how that silences the negative thoughts
you had!

---

*I praise You, Jesus, because of who You are. You are amazing,
and You deserve all of my worship and thanks. Thank You
for giving me praise as a tool to silence the enemy!*

TOSSED ASIDE

Jesus said to [the religious leaders], "Have you not read in the
Holy Writings, 'The Stone that was put aside by the workmen
has become the most important Stone in the building?
The Lord has done this. We think it is great!' "

MATTHEW 21:42

Have you ever felt tossed aside or forgotten? Have you ever been left
out at recess? Jesus knows exactly what this feels like. God's Word tells
us that Jesus was rejected. He had some friends and followers, but most
people rejected Him and sent Him to die on a cross. The crowds called
for Jesus to be crucified. They humiliated Him. It's hard to imagine how
difficult this must have been for Jesus. He endured all of it out of His deep
love for us. Men rejected Jesus, but God had chosen Him. Remember
this the next time you feel alone or forgotten. God chose you to be His
much-loved child. Jesus sees everything that is happening to you, and He
understands your heart. He is with you. He will help you face whatever
bad thing might come, and He will surprise you with blessings along
the way. Remember God's promise to turn bad things into good ones
(Romans 8:28)! You are never alone.

Jesus, help me remember You are with me when I'm feeling alone.
Thank You for loving and understanding me. I'm sorry You
were rejected. I'm choosing to love You and follow You.

THE GREAT WEDDING

" 'Go out into the roads and as many people as you can find,
ask them to come to the wedding supper.' "

MATTHEW 22:9

Jesus told His followers another picture story about the great wedding.
He's talking again about the kingdom of God. Guess what? We're all
invited! Do you like to get invitations to birthday parties? It's so fun
to see an invitation and know that it's for you! In this story, Jesus said
that the guests needed to have their wedding clothes on. If they weren't
dressed for the wedding, they would get tossed out of the wedding
reception. Remember that Jesus' picture stories always had deeper
meaning. What Jesus meant here was that none of us can get to heaven
unless we're dressed in the righteousness of Christ. What does that
mean? Righteousness means "rightness" or perfect-ness. But no one is
perfect except Jesus. He never ever sinned, and yet He was punished for
our sins so that we can be with God. And we can't get into heaven unless
we ask Jesus to put His righteousness on us so that when God looks at
us, He sees what Jesus did for us on the cross instead of our sin. Are you
dressed for the great wedding?

Jesus, I ask You to cover me up with your perfection!
Thank You for taking my sin and dressing me for the
great wedding where I can be with You forever!

GOD'S WORD

Jesus said to [the religious leaders], "You are wrong because you do not know the Holy Writings or the power of God."
MATTHEW 22:29

The Bible is a powerful tool for the followers of Jesus. Did you know that God's Word is alive? Hebrews 4:12 tells us this: "God's word is alive and working. It is sharper than a sword sharpened on both sides. It cuts all the way into us, where the soul and the spirit are joined. It cuts to the center of our joints and our bones. And God's word judges the thoughts and feelings in our hearts" (ICB). God's Word can take a look inside our hearts and help us know right from wrong. The Bible also calls God's Word a sword that we can use to defeat the enemy's lies. Jesus wants us to know His Word. Psalm 119:11 tells us to hide God's Word in our hearts so that we won't sin. How can you hide God's Word in your heart? First you need to read it. Make a habit of getting into God's Word every day. Open your Bible and find a daily devotional like this one. Read the scriptures and try to memorize them whenever you can. The Holy Spirit actually helps you learn the words of Jesus and remember them when you need them!

Jesus, thank You for the Bible! It is a gift and a blessing. Help me come to know and love Your words.

BE LIKE JESUS 101

Jesus said to [the proud religious law-keeper], " 'You must love the
Lord your God with all your heart and with all your soul and with all
your mind.' This is the first and greatest of the Laws. The second
is like it, 'You must love your neighbor as you love yourself.' "

MATTHEW 22:37–39

What am I supposed to do with my life? Get good grades in school? Go
on to college? Start a family? That's what the majority of people in this
world consider their purpose, also known as the American Dream! Those
are all great goals, but is that really what God wants from us? Check out
what 1 Corinthians 13:1–3 tells us: "If I could speak all the languages of
earth and of angels, but didn't love others, I would only be a noisy gong
or a clanging cymbal. . . . If I understood all of God's secret plans. . .and
if I had such faith that I could move mountains, but didn't love others, I
would be nothing. If I gave everything I have to the poor. . .I could boast
about it, but if I didn't love others, I would have gained nothing" (NLT).
Basically, we could achieve the American dream and so much more, but
it would all count for nothing if we didn't do it out of love for Jesus and
for others! God's purpose for us might not be easy, but it is simple: Love
Him and love others.

Jesus, please change my heart to match Your purpose for my life.
Help me to work hard in all things out of my love for You!

OTHERS COME FIRST

"The person who is not trying to honor
himself will be made important."

MATTHEW 23:12

Have you noticed the theme in Jesus' words? We love others by serving them. The first shall be last, and the last shall be first. The humble person will be lifted up. Being great comes from serving others. This is completely upside down from what our world believes now. Many kids today are focused on how many likes they can get on their social media accounts or YouTube videos. They're upset when they don't get enough traffic to their posts. But Jesus says here that the person who is not trying to get the most attention will be made important. The kids scrambling to try and become famous aren't living the life Jesus wants for them. Think of the word *joy*. The key to finding joy in your heart is **J**esus first, **O**thers next, and **Y**ourself last. The first letter of each word spells out *JOY*! If you spend your life in the service of Jesus and others, you will find that your heart is overflowing with joy. And it won't matter how many likes you get from people you don't even know!

Jesus, please forgive me when I worry about how many people like me or the things I do. I want to find joy in serving You and others. Help me overflow with joy so that others know it comes from You.

73

PRETENDING

"It is bad for you, teachers of the Law and proud religious law-keepers, you who pretend to be someone you are not! You clean the outside of the cup and plate, but leave the inside full of strong bad desires and are not able to keep from doing sinful things."

MATTHEW 23:25

Playing make-believe can be fun! Isn't it exciting to dress up in a costume and go to a party? That's not the kind of pretending Jesus is talking about here. The Pharisees were getting a strong talking-to from Jesus! He knew their hearts, and they were dark on the inside. The Pharisees knew all about God and the Old Testament rules. They did their best to look good and religious in front of everyone. They wanted the people to think highly of them. But inside they had evil in their hearts. Jesus said it's like cleaning your cups and plates and shining up the outsides but forgetting that last night's dinner is still stuck inside them! You wouldn't eat out of that, would you? Gross! That's what Jesus saw when he looked at the Pharisees. Something gross and fake. They were pretending to love and honor God, but it was all a lie. Ask Jesus to look on the inside of You and wash you clean. He will!

Jesus, please make me clean on the inside before I worry about the outside. I never want to pretend about my love for You.

LET JESUS COMFORT YOU

[Jesus said to the Jews,] "How many times I wanted to gather
your children around Me, as a chicken gathers her young
ones under her wings. But you would not let Me."

MATTHEW 23:37

Think about the last time you were really sad. Can you remember why you felt that way? Jesus says He wants to comfort His followers. He wants to comfort you! Have you ever seen a mommy chicken with her babies? A mommy chicken clucks and flaps her wings to encourage her babies to run to her and gather under her wings so that she can protect them from harm. Can you picture Jesus doing that for you when you are sad? Go ahead and give it a try! Jesus created your imagination, and He wants to use it for His glory. Ask Jesus to show you a picture of Him comforting you! Can you see Jesus in your mind? What is He doing? Draw a picture of what Jesus showed you so that you will always remember that He is with you. Psalm 34:18 says, "The LORD is close to the brokenhearted and saves those who are crushed in spirit" (NIV). Write one of these verses on your picture and hang it where you'll see it often.

*Jesus, thank You for using my imagination to speak to me.
It makes me so happy that You want to comfort me when I am sad!*

THE WRONG WAY

Jesus said to [His followers], "Be careful that
no one leads you the wrong way."

MATTHEW 24:4

Jesus told us that many will come in His name claiming to know Him
or even to *be* Jesus. This has happened in our current history. This still
happens in the church. People claim to have all the answers about Jesus,
but they don't. You'll have lots of teachers at church as you grow up.
Make sure to listen to the Holy Spirit speaking to you as you learn from
other people. If a teacher is leading you in a wrong way, the Holy Spirit
is alive inside of you and will often give you a warning signal. Something
will just feel a little "off." Don't automatically believe everything someone
tries to teach you about Jesus and His ways. How will you know for sure
if someone is teaching you something wrong? Ask Jesus and seek truth
from Him in the Bible. Whenever you get the "warning signal," do a
search in God's Word. Look up the answers and ask Jesus to help you
know what is right and wrong. Psalm 32:8 says that God "will instruct
you and teach you in the way you should go" (NIV).

*Jesus, thank You that I can depend on You to teach me right from
wrong. Help me learn to hear the Holy Spirit's warning signal!
Please give me wisdom to search out Your Words for myself.*

COMING IN THE CLOUDS

"[All nations] will see the Son of Man coming in the clouds
of the sky with power and shining-greatness."
MATTHEW 24:30

Seeing Jesus coming on the clouds is the great hope of all believers. It's
what we are patiently waiting for. We're waiting for the day when Jesus
comes, rids the world of evil forever, and wipes away all tears and sadness,
and we get to spend eternity with Him. We were made for another world
where Jesus Christ is King forever. That's why some things will always
feel wrong and sad here. We were made to live in a sin-free world with
Jesus. But Jesus tells us that no one knows when this is going to happen,
so don't let anyone fool you into thinking that they know. It's important
to live every day like Jesus could be coming back this very day, because
He could! But until you see Jesus coming in the clouds, keep talking to
Jesus and loving others. Is there anything you would do differently if you
knew Jesus was coming back today?

---

*Jesus, I'm so excited to know You are coming back to make all things
right in this dark world! No more sadness and hurting people! I can
hardly wait! Help me live for You patiently as I wait for Your return.*

A GOOD AND FAITHFUL SERVANT

"His owner said to [the servant who doubled his five pieces of money], 'You have done well. You are a good and faithful servant. You have been faithful over a few things. I will put many things in your care. Come and share my joy.'"

MATTHEW 25:21

As you know by now, Jesus loved to tell picture stories. We call this parable in Matthew 25 the parable of the talents. In Bible times, a talent was known as a large sum of money. A landowner was going on a long trip, so he divided up his money and gave it to his servants according to their abilities. One servant was given five talents, another servant was given two talents, and the last one was given one talent. The man who was given five talents went right to work with that money and earned five more. The one who was given two talents earned two more. But the last servant was afraid that something bad would happen to his talents, so he buried them and didn't earn a thing. He did nothing for his master and got in trouble for it. This parable had a double meaning. Can you think about what this means for your life? Jesus has given each of us certain gifts and talents, and He wants us to use them to honor God and bless others. How are you using the gifts God has given you?

Jesus, I want to be Your good and faithful servant.
Teach me how to use my gifts to bless You and others.

SERVING JESUS

" 'For I was hungry and you gave Me food to eat. I was thirsty
and you gave Me water to drink. I was a stranger
and you gave Me a room.' "

MATTHEW 25:35

Did you know that when we serve others, we are actually serving Jesus?
Serving someone else means that you put that person's needs above
your own; you find out what they need, and you do your best to help
them. Jesus was telling His disciples that people who serve others will
be welcomed into the kingdom of heaven because they are really serving
Jesus. Matthew 25:40 says, "Truly I tell you, whatever you did for one
of the least of these brothers and sisters of mine, you did for me" (NIV).
When you see someone in need, can you picture Jesus being the one in
need instead? Think of families at Christmastime who don't have money
to buy any gifts. What if it was Jesus who had no gifts? Could you find a
way to help? Sit down with your family and think about ways you can get
involved with needy people in your community. Most communities have
a soup kitchen, and many churches stock up on supplies to help people
in need. Find out how you can help, and remember that you are serving
Jesus as you do it!

Jesus, I want to help take care of needs in my community.
Thank You for Your blessings! Help me share
these blessings with those in need.

NO MATTER WHAT OTHERS THINK

A woman came with a jar of perfume. She had given much money
for this. As Jesus ate, she poured the perfume on His head.
MATTHEW 26:7

Jesus was at the home of Simon the Leper when His friend Mary
came and poured expensive perfume on His head. The disciples didn't
understand what she was doing and thought that the money could have
been better spent feeding the poor. Jesus defended Mary and told the
disciples that she had done a beautiful thing. She was preparing Jesus
for burial, something they couldn't yet understand. Mary believed that
she needed to pour her expensive perfume on Jesus even if other people
thought she was weird or wasteful for doing such a strange thing. She
knew that what she was doing would honor Jesus. So she did it no matter
what anyone else thought of her. Sometimes it's hard to do something we
believe Jesus is asking us to do. But Jesus will defend you and take care
of you as you carry out His plans for your life. Jesus said that this special
story of Mary would be told all throughout the world, and you're hearing
it right now too.

---

*Jesus, help me to be strong and confident in my faith as I live
my life for You—even when other people think my faith
is strange or weird. I know You are with me.*

NOT WHAT I WANT,
BUT WHAT GOD WANTS

[Jesus] went on a little farther and got down with His face on the ground. He prayed, "My Father, if it can be done, take away what is before Me. Even so, not what I want but what You want."

MATTHEW 26:39

Jesus was coming to His last days on earth. He knew He would soon be betrayed and sent to the cross for the sins of the whole world. He knew that He would be separated from His Father. He knew that He would face torture and death. He asked God if there was another way. But there wasn't. The only way for us to be with our holy God for eternity was for a perfect human to take the punishment for our sin. And that's what Jesus came to do. It was the only way for us to be saved. All of us have sinned, and none of us are perfect. But Jesus is perfect. And Jesus makes it possible for us to have a relationship with our heavenly Father. Jesus was able to say, "Not what I want but what You want," to His Father. Jesus gives us the courage to follow God even when it's hard. We can say to God, "Not what I want but what You want," when it comes to our own selfish desires.

Jesus, thank You for taking the punishment for my sins.
Please give me courage to do difficult things as I follow You.

BE BOLD FOR JESUS

Peter remembered the words Jesus had said to him,
"Before a rooster crows, you will say three times you do
not know Me." Peter went outside and cried with loud cries.
MATTHEW 26:75

Jesus told the disciples that they would end up falling away and disowning Him. To *disown* means to say that you do not belong to someone. The disciples told Jesus they would never disown Him. Peter even told Jesus that He would die before he disowned Jesus. But the disciples didn't know how awful things were about to get. Jesus told Peter about the rooster. Jesus was soon betrayed and arrested. The people wanted Jesus put to death. Peter was asked publicly if he was one of Jesus' followers, and he denied it because he was afraid. In fact, he was asked three different times if he was a follower of Jesus, and three times he denied it. Then the rooster crowed and Peter remembered Jesus' words. Peter went out and cried in shame. Our words don't count for much unless our actions follow. Jesus loved Peter even though He knew Peter would deny Him. He loves us too. He also wants to help us be bold in our faith so that we can share freely how much God loves and cares for us.

---

*Jesus, help me to be bold for You. Please give me courage
to stand up for truth and share my faith whenever possible.*

WHY DID JESUS DIE?

After they had made fun of [Jesus], they took the coat off
and put His own clothes on Him. Then they led
Him away to be nailed to a cross.
MATTHEW 27:31

God is holy and perfect in all of His ways. Psalm 145:17 says, "The LORD is righteous in all his ways and faithful in all he does" (NIV). We are not. We sin. We mess up. We've all made lots of mistakes. We can't understand everything about God or His ways, but we do know that we can't get to God if we aren't perfect. That's why Jesus came! God made us and loves us very much, and He made each of us with the ability to make our own choices. We can choose to live in our sins, forever separated from God. Or we can choose to accept the righteousness (perfect-ness) of Jesus and be with God for eternity. Jesus died to take our sins so that when God looks at us, He sees the perfect sacrifice that Jesus made for us instead. Second Corinthians 5:21 explains it this way: "Christ had no sin. But God made him become sin. God did this for us so that in Christ we could become right with God" (ICB). Jesus came and died so that we can be made perfect before God. It was the only way.

Jesus, I don't understand everything about You, but I accept
You as my sacrifice. I love You because You loved me first.

WHEN JESUS DIED

Then Jesus gave another loud cry and gave up His spirit and died.
At once the curtain in the house of God was torn in two from top
to bottom. The earth shook and the rocks fell apart. Graves were
opened. Bodies of many of God's people who were dead were raised.
MATTHEW 27:50–52

When Jesus died, several miraculous things happened. First, it had turned very dark outside in the middle of the day. Then, at the very moment when Jesus took His last breath, the curtain inside the temple in Jerusalem was miraculously torn in two from top to bottom. This curtain closing off the Holy of Holies was a big deal because only the high priest was allowed to go behind it once a year to make a sacrifice for the sins of all people. God tore the curtain from top to bottom because He wanted people to know that Jesus had now made a way for all believers to enter the holy place to come to God. Jesus is the only sacrifice ever needed. Because of His death for us, all believers have access to God all the time. Then an earthquake happened and graves were opened. People who were dead came back to life! Matthew 27:54 says, "The captain of the soldiers and those with him who were watching Jesus, saw all the things that were happening. They saw the earth shake and they were very much afraid. They said, 'For sure, this Man was the Son of God.' " The people who hadn't believed in Jesus only moments earlier saw these miracles take place and knew that Jesus was telling the truth about Himself.

---

*Jesus, I believe You are who You say You are.
I put all my trust in You.*

MIRACLE IN THE TOMB

The next day, the day after Jesus was killed, the head religious
leaders and the proud religious law-keepers gathered together
in front of Pilate. They said, "Sir, we remember what that
Man Who fooled people said when He was living,
'After three days I am to rise from the dead.'"

MATTHEW 27:62–63

Jesus wasn't trying to fool anybody! He really did rise from the dead after
three days. It's a historical fact. Jesus appeared many times to many people
over a forty-day period before He went back to heaven. People saw Him
die, and they saw Him after He came back to life! The Pharisees didn't
understand what Jesus had done, and they were afraid of His power, so
they posted guards to watch the tomb after He was killed. They were
worried that some of Jesus' followers would come and take the body and
pretend He came back to life. They even put a special seal on the tomb
to keep anyone from going in or out. But they couldn't stop God's power.
Jesus was alive! He proved that He was the Son of God, and everything
He claimed came true. The same power that raised Jesus from the dead is
the power that is offered to each of us who believe. Jesus proved that He
can conquer death, and that death on this earth is not the end. We have
the promise of eternal life in resurrected bodies, with Jesus.

You are alive, Jesus! I'm so thankful that
You are alive and at work in me!

JESUS IS WHO HE SAYS HE IS

The angel said to the women, "Do not be afraid. I know you are
looking for Jesus Who was nailed to the cross. He is not here!
He has risen from the dead as He said He would.
Come and see the place where the Lord lay."

MATTHEW 28:5–6

Two women went to see Jesus' grave at the beginning of the week. But
a violent earthquake stopped them in their tracks. An angel came down
from heaven, pushed the stone away from Jesus' tomb, and sat on it.
The soldiers guarding the tomb were terrified. The angel tried to calm
the women and announced the Good News. Jesus is alive! He is who He
says He is! The angel invited them in to see where Jesus' body had lain.
Then He urged them to go and tell the disciples that Jesus was alive. The
women ran to find them. They were scared but full of joy too! And then
a most amazing thing happened. They saw Jesus Himself! He appeared
to the women, and they bowed down and worshipped Him. He told
them not to be afraid. He had truly come back to life! The guards who
were watching the tomb went and reported what happened to the chief
priests. They came up with a lie so people wouldn't believe that Jesus
really came back to life. But God was bigger than their lie, and the truth
always wins.

Jesus, Your story is so amazing and powerful!
Thank You that I serve a living God!

HE'S ALWAYS WITH US

Jesus came and said to [His disciples], "All power has been given to Me in heaven and on earth. Go and make followers of all the nations. Baptize them in the name of the Father and of the Son and of the Holy Spirit. Teach them to do all the things I have told you. And I am with you always, even to the end of the world."

MATTHEW 28:18–20

These famous last words of Jesus are also known as the Great Commission. A *commission* is when you trust someone else to do a task with special power and authority. This commission was for the disciples, but it is also for us today. Jesus wants us to share His love with everyone and pass on the truth of Jesus to them. The disciples knew that the power of Jesus was real, and so they went and did as Jesus asked. They shared about Jesus, and the Gospel was made known worldwide and is still being made known to this day. Jesus promised to be with them always, and He promises the same thing to us. Jesus sent us His Holy Spirit to be alive in us always. Are you sharing the Great Commission? Ask Jesus for help and courage to do what He has asked.

Jesus, thank You for Your promise to always be with me. Give me help and courage to share about You with those around me.

JESUS IS GREATER
THAN ANY FEAR

Jesus healed those who were sick of many kinds of diseases.
He put out many demons. Jesus would not allow the
demons to speak because they knew Who He was.

MARK 1:34

Have you ever had a bad dream? Or maybe there's something that you're kind of afraid of: a dark basement or being alone in your room. I have great news for you! Jesus can take all of those fears and turn them into something good! The Bible tells us that even just the name of Jesus has power! Philippians 2:10 tells us "that at the name of Jesus every knee should bow, in heaven and on earth and under the earth" (NIV). Jesus is always bigger than anything that might try to scare you. If you are having a bad dream or if you find yourself alone in a dark place, you don't have to say a long prayer. You can simply say the name of Jesus! Sometimes that alone is the best prayer we can pray. When we call on Jesus' name, we're asking Him to take our fears and fill us with His love. Darkness has to leave when Jesus enters. First John 4:4 tells us, "You belong to God, my dear children. You have already won a victory over those people, because the Spirit who lives in you is greater than the spirit who lives in the world" (NLT).

Jesus, I trust that there is power in Your name.
Thank You for rescuing me from fear.

A DAY OF REST

"The Day of Rest was made for the good of man.
Man was not made for the Day of Rest."

MARK 2:27

God gave us a good example to follow from the very beginning. After He created the world, He rested. He didn't have to. He chose to. Now, you probably gave up naps years ago, but parents still need them sometimes! Many grown-ups who work in an office work five days a week and have the weekend free. Their bosses know that rest helps them be better workers when they come back. God made us and knows that our bodies need rest. In years past, the day of rest happened on Sunday and businesses would be closed. Today things are a bit different. Our world is fast paced, and people are constantly working or using social media. But Jesus calls us to do things His way. Although it's hard to go against the flow of our world and rest, Jesus says that it is important for us to slow down and take time to refresh our bodies and our minds. Talk with your family and come up with a plan to limit your activities and screen time on Sunday or on a day of the week that works for your family. Then do something relaxing that brings you joy and peace instead of homework and screen time.

---

*Jesus, help me to rest my brain
and my body so that I can be refreshed.*

EVERYONE WAS HEALED

Wherever [Jesus] went, they would lay the sick people in the
streets in the center of town where people gather. They begged
Him that they might touch the bottom of His coat. Everyone who
did was healed. This happened in the towns and in the
cities and in the country where He went.

MARK 6:56

The book of Mark starts with Jesus' life and ministry. Mark shows us that
Jesus was a man of action. He practiced what He preached. Wherever
Jesus went, crowds of people followed. They knew Jesus had the power to
heal. The crowds would lay sick people in the streets for Jesus to touch.
The sick believed that if they just touched the bottom of His robe they
would be healed. Imagine people who had been sick their whole lives
desperate to be free of their illness. Imagine blind people and people
who couldn't walk discovering that they could be healed. They didn't
completely understand Jesus' power, but they wanted to be well. Jesus
knew the state of their hearts, and He had loving compassion for them.
He could have healed everyone on earth instantly, but He waited for the
people to come to Him by faith. Jesus is still healing people today in
much the same way. He waits for us to come to Him.

---

*Jesus, I trust You to give me and my loved ones what we need. You
know what is best for us. Thank You for Your healing power.*

THE DEAF HEAR AND
THE MUTE SPEAK

*"[Jesus] makes those who could not hear so they can hear.
He makes those who could not speak so they can speak."*

MARK 7:37

Jesus continued to heal the people who were brought to Him. One day someone brought Him a man who couldn't hear and could barely talk. Jesus put His fingers into the man's ears and then touched his tongue and said, "Be opened!" The man was healed. He could hear, and he was able to talk like anyone else. Jesus can still open ears and mouths today. While He can heal people physically, He can also heal them spiritually. Some people who have been hurt by others often blame God. Some people refuse to believe there even is a God. And some people believe God is real but that He is too busy to care about them. But the God who could make the deaf hear and the mute speak can still cause those people to hear today. God's Spirit is still powerfully at work in our hearts and in our world. If you know people who seem far from God, pray. Pray that God would open their ears to believe that Jesus is real and that they would ask Jesus to be Lord of their life.

---

*Jesus, I trust that You still have power to heal people's hearts,
minds, and bodies. I pray for _____,
that You would be real to them too.*

BE SALTY

"Salt is good. But if salt loses its taste, how can it be made
to taste like salt again? Have salt in yourselves
and be at peace with each other."

MARK 9:50

Do you like french fries? Who doesn't? But have you ever tried french fries without salt? They are bland and definitely don't taste as good. The Bible has a couple of things to say about salt. Colossians 4:6 says, "Let your conversation be always full of grace, seasoned with salt, so that you may know how to answer everyone" (NIV). When we talk to our friends and family about Jesus, He wants our conversations to be respectful and loving—sprinkled with grace like salt on french fries. When we are kind and loving as we talk about Jesus, people will want to know more. No one will want to keep talking with us or hear what we have to say in the future if we are bossy and rude or come across like a know-it-all. Do you like to hang around people like that? When we have grace for others, we act and think with forgiveness and kindness toward them. How can you sprinkle more grace in your conversations?

Jesus, please help me to sprinkle more grace on people when I'm talking to them about You. I want to be loving and kind. Thank You for Your never-ending grace for me!

OLD AND YOUNG

[Jesus] took the children in His arms. He put His hands
on them and prayed that good would come to them.

MARK 10:16

Criticism is when someone judges you, usually in a negative way. People were often criticizing Jesus because they thought He should be doing what they wanted Him to do. The Pharisees, and sometimes even Jesus' own friends, were critical of the people He chose to spend time with. Back in Bible times, women and children weren't considered very important. In fact, they were often treated as property. This was not God's plan for women or children. Jesus came to show another way. He loved women and children and spent lots of time with them. Jesus was offended when the disciples tried to keep children away from Him. He stood up for children and told the disciples not to prevent kids from coming. He honored women and children and made them feel important. He said that "anyone who will not receive the kingdom of God like a little child will never enter it." The faith of children is pure and strong. They believe someone who feels safe to them. Jesus wants all of His children, old and young, to have faith like that!

---

*I'm so thankful that I'm important to You, Jesus. Your love for me
is amazing! Help me to keep my faith strong and
pure. I know I'm safe with You.*

WISE LEADERSHIP

Jesus stopped and told them to call the blind man. They called to
him and said, "Take hope! Stand up, He is calling for you!"

MARK 10:49

A wise leader once said that the best leaders walk slowly through the
crowd. They take time to get to know the people around them. They don't
race from one thing to the next, ignoring people on their way. The first
thing we notice in this scripture is that Jesus stopped. Jesus was with
His disciples, and a large crowd of people were there too. They were all
walking together out of the city. But Jesus stopped to pay attention to one
blind beggar who was sitting beside the road. The beggar was calling to
Jesus to have mercy on Him. Jesus stopped and listened. When He called
for the blind beggar to come to Him, the man jumped up and went to
Jesus. Jesus healed him, and the man followed Jesus along the road. The
Bible tells us that many who were there that day told the blind beggar to
be quiet and stop calling out for Jesus. But Jesus had compassion on this
poor man and reached out to Him. A wise leader does what God wants
them to do, not what the crowd wants them to do. As you grow up, how
can you become a better leader?

---

*Jesus, help me to be a wise leader like You. Help me listen to others
and have compassion for them no matter what the crowd says.*

TELL EVERYONE

[Jesus] said to them, "You are to go to all the world
and preach the Good News to every person."
MARK 16:15

Just like in the book of Matthew, we see Jesus give the Great Commission to His followers. Remember what that means? It's when you trust someone else with special power and authority to complete a task. The book of Mark gives us a little more detail. It tells of the power that Jesus gives us when we believe in His name. The Holy Spirit comes to live inside our hearts and works in us to carry out God's plans here on earth. Jesus wants us to tell everyone about this great power! Ephesians 1:19–20 says, "I [Paul] also pray that you will understand the incredible greatness of God's power for us who believe him. This is the same mighty power that raised Christ from the dead and seated him in the place of honor at God's right hand in the heavenly realms" (NLT). This power is what is alive and working inside of you today. Isn't that amazing? How can you begin telling everyone about the great power and love of Jesus? Sit down with your family and brainstorm ideas to share God's love with those around you.

Jesus, thank You for the power of Your Holy Spirit living inside
of me. Please fill my heart with Your love and courage
as I tell everyone about Your great love for them.

HOPE FOR THE HOPELESS

When the Lord saw [the woman whose son had died], He had
loving-pity for her and said, "Do not cry." He went and put His hand
on the box in which the dead man was carried. The men who were
carrying it, stopped. Jesus said, "Young man, I say to you,
get up!" The man who was dead sat up and began
to talk. Then Jesus gave him to his mother.

Luke 7:13–15

Jesus was again walking with a large crowd and witnessed another
desperate situation. A young man, the only son of a widow, was dead, and
his body was being carried through the town. Because the main wage
earner in the family had died, the widow was probably going to have a
lot of financial problems in the future. She was sad and probably scared.
But what could be done? Her son was already dead. But then Jesus saw
her. The Bible tells us that His heart went out to her. He had compassion
and love for this widow who had lost her only son. He told her not to
cry and then He commanded the dead man to get up. Jesus can take a
completely hopeless situation and turn it around. Whenever you feel like
a problem is completely impossible, reach out to Jesus. Trust that He can
do the impossible and bring hope to hopeless situations.

---

*Jesus, help me to trust that You can bring hope to any
situation. Show me how to share this hope
with my friends and family members.*

THE GOOD SAMARITAN

"Which of these three do you think was a neighbor to the man
who was beaten by the robbers?" The man who knew the Law
said, "The one who showed loving-pity on him."
Then Jesus said, "Go and do the same."
LUKE 10:36–37

One day a religious expert asked Jesus a question as a test. He wanted to hear an explanation about who his neighbor was. Instead of answering this question outright and falling into the expert's trap, Jesus told him a story that we call the parable of the good Samaritan. A man was beaten and left for dead by robbers. Three people walked by the hurting man. The first two saw the man and passed by on the other side. The third man went to the wounded man and helped him. He bandaged his wounds and took him to an inn to heal, paying for his expenses. Which man acted like a good neighbor to the wounded man? The one who helped, of course. What does this story mean to you? Who is your neighbor? Is it just your friends and the people you love? No, Jesus says that anyone we come across is our neighbor. And Jesus wants us to love our neighbors as ourselves. Sometimes that is difficult! Especially if you have unfriendly neighbors! But Jesus can help you love even the unlovable. Just ask!

---

*Jesus, please help me love my neighbors in ways
that bless You. Even when it's hard.*

MARY'S CHOICE

Jesus said to her, "Martha, Martha, you are worried and
troubled about many things. Only a few things are important,
even just one. Mary has chosen the good thing.
It will not be taken away from her."

LUKE 10:41–42

Jesus went to visit Mary and Martha. Martha was so excited to have Jesus
visit her home that she went to work right away, getting the house ready
for guests. But her sister, Mary, chose to sit down at the feet of Jesus and
listen to all He had to say. Martha realized what was happening and was
upset that she had to do all the work herself! She complained to Jesus
about Mary's lack of help. But Jesus defended Mary and told Martha
that her sister had made the better choice by choosing to be with Jesus
instead of just doing work for Him. Have you ever volunteered at church
before? Sometimes we get so distracted by the work we're doing *for* Jesus
that we forget to take time to be *with* Jesus. That's what happened with
Martha. She loved Jesus and was very happy to have Him in her home,
but she got distracted by all the work. What do you get distracted by?
Ask Jesus to help you get rid of distractions so that you can have some
quiet, focused time with Him every day.

---

*Jesus, help me to make the best choice like Mary did.
I want to serve You, but I need to be with You more.*

PRAY LIKE JESUS

Jesus said to [His disciples], "When you pray, say, 'Our Father in heaven, Your name is holy. May Your holy nation come. What You want done, may it be done on earth as it is in heaven. Give us the bread we need everyday. Forgive us our sins, as we forgive those who sin against us. Do not let us be tempted.' "

LUKE 11:2–4

Jesus gave us a great example of how to pray to God. He begins this prayer by praising God. By worshipping and praising God first, we unlock our feelings of gratitude and thanksgiving. When we get our eyes off of ourselves and what we want God to do for us, we are happier and more content. Then we ask Jesus to meet our needs, which are very different from wants. Prayer is a two-way conversation, not like giving God a Christmas list of things we want. Then we ask for forgiveness for mistakes we've made that might be festering. And we allow Jesus to shine a light in our hearts on who we might need to forgive. And finally, we ask for God's spiritual protection to keep us away from evil and temptation. God loves our conversations with Him. We don't always have to pray the same way; we can talk to God about anything. These are just good ideas to remember as we talk to God.

Jesus, thank You for teaching us how to pray. Help me to stop and listen as I talk to God. Help me learn to hear Your voice.

TALKING TO GOD

"If he keeps on asking, he will get up
and give him as much as he needs."
LUKE 11:8

Jesus tells a story about a man whose family is already in bed when a friend comes and asks for a favor in the middle of the night. No one wants to get up in the middle of the night unless it's an emergency. If someone keeps on knocking persistently, we will likely get up to see what they need. Jesus also wants us to knock on the door of heaven persistently—that is, He wants us to keep on asking Him for things in prayer until we receive what we ask for. He wants us to show faith and not give up. The book of Luke shows Jesus praying—a lot! He is persistent in prayer. He has a regular rhythm of prayer. Philippians 4:6–7 tells us this: "Don't worry about anything; instead, pray about everything. Tell God what you need, and thank him for all he has done. Then you will experience God's peace, which exceeds anything we can understand. His peace will guard your hearts and minds as you live in Christ Jesus" (NLT). Here is a promise to remember your whole life! When you get in the habit of praying instead of worrying, God fills you with His peace.

---

*Jesus, I want to get into a regular habit of talking to You
about everything. I know You will fill me with Your
peace when I pray instead of worrying.*

WHAT KIND OF LIGHT
DO YOU SHINE?

"The eye is the light of the body. When your eye is good, your whole
body is full of light. When your eye is sinful, your whole body is
full of darkness. Be careful that the light in you is not dark.
If your whole body is full of light, with no dark part,
then it will shine. It will be as a lamp that gives light."

LUKE 11:34–36

There is a lot of darkness in this world, and the enemy wants to load up your brain with it. Imagine you're at school in the gymnasium at night for some reason, maybe at a basketball game or a choir concert. And suddenly the lights go out. Your whole school is completely dark, and you can't see anyone. Some people even start to panic. Then someone opens up their little flashlight app on their phone and a small light is seen. People begin to calm down because they can see light again. When we choose to follow Jesus, He shines His light in our hearts for all to see. Just like everyone can see the one little flashlight when all the lights go out, you can be a source of light in the darkness that surrounds you every day.

---

*Jesus, protect me from the darkness around me. Help me choose
to make right choices when it comes to what I look at
and allow in my mind. Fill me with Your light.*

JUST THINGS

Then Jesus said to them all, "Watch yourselves! Keep from
wanting all kinds of things you should not have. A man's
life is not made up of things, even if he has many riches."

LUKE 12:15

If you woke up tomorrow morning and one of your favorite toys was broken, you would be pretty sad. It's okay to be sad about things like that. Sometimes things are important to us for a reason. Still, it's important to remember they are only *things*. You can look around your home and find a ton more things to be thankful for! Plus you have your family and friends and church family! People are always more important than things. Hebrews 13:5 says, "Keep your lives free from the love of money and be content with what you have, because God has said, 'Never will I leave you; never will I forsake you' " (NIV). Money and things are pretty much worshipped in our culture. When people don't know the love of Jesus, they try to fill up the emptiness in their lives with things. When we learn not to worship things or money, we become content with what we have.

*Jesus, please remind me that my things are just things.
Help me be content with what You've given me and
thankful for the blessings You have in store for me.*

CLOTHES AND FOOD

Jesus said to His followers, ". . .do not worry about your life, what you are going to eat. Do not worry about your body, what you are going to wear. Life is worth more than food. The body is worth more than clothes."

Luke 12:22–23

Open up your Bible to Luke 12 and read verses 22–32. Jesus gives us good examples of why we shouldn't worry. Jesus tells us about birds and flowers. Think about the birds in your neighborhood. They don't have jobs. They don't have a kitchen to make food for their families. But God feeds them! And think of the flowers. They don't have any money to buy clothes, and yet they are stunningly beautiful. God dresses them Himself. Jesus tells us that we are more valuable to God than birds and flowers. We're His favorite! So of course He is going to take care of us. Having nice clothes and eating yummy food is fine as long as it's not our life purpose. Jesus wants our life purpose to match up with His purpose for our lives: to love God and love others. Worrying about things like food and clothes shows that we don't trust Jesus enough to take care of our needs. Talk to Him about this.

Jesus, help me to trust You with my basic needs like food and clothes. Help me not to be obsessed with having and getting more.

THE LOST SON

"While [the younger son] was yet a long way off, his father saw
him. The father was full of loving-pity for him. He ran
and threw his arms around him and kissed him."

LUKE 15:20

Jesus gave us the story of the prodigal son. *Prodigal* means reckless or
wasteful. The son asked the father to give him his inheritance early. So the
young man took it and left the country to waste his money on whatever
he felt like. Pretty soon he was out of food and completely broke. The
young man had come to the lowest point of his life. He knew he had
nothing left to do but go crawling back to his dad and beg forgiveness.
He wasn't expecting to be treated like a son anymore because he was
ashamed at what he'd done and certain his father would be upset. But
Jesus said that the father was watching for his son to return. He was full
of love and compassion for his son, and he ran out to meet him while he
was still a long way off. His father celebrated the return of his lost son,
forgiving him completely. Jesus told us this story to show how God feels
about us when we come to Him. He waits patiently for us, and then He
blesses us with His love.

---

*Jesus, thank You for loving me even when I've made mistakes.
You patiently wait for me to come to You, and then You fill
me with Your love. Help me to love others like that too.*

THE WAY JESUS FORGIVES

"Watch yourselves! If your brother sins, speak sharp words to him.
If he is sorry and turns from his sin, forgive him. What if he sins
against you seven times in one day? If he comes to you and
says he is sorry and turns from his sin, forgive him."

LUKE 17:3–4

Jesus wants us to be quick to forgive. This doesn't mean we have to trust a person who sins against us over and over again. Trust and forgiveness are different. Forgiveness means we let go of the issue and allow God to deal with it. When we carry unforgiveness in our hearts, it gets really heavy. That's called bitterness. And when we hang on to bitterness, it can mess up all of our other relationships too. So how can you be quick to forgive? As soon as something happens that hurts you, take it straight to Jesus. Tell Him how you feel and ask Him to give you His thoughts about it. He will help you to feel His supernatural love for the person who hurt you. Then you can let it go and ask Jesus for wisdom on what to say and do. Remember, though, if someone hurt you and is bothering you over and over again, make sure to tell a grown-up whom you trust. They can help you deal wisely with the situation.

Jesus, I confess that sometimes it's hard for me to forgive. Help me to see other people through Your eyes and to forgive them quickly.

HEAVEN ON THE INSIDE

Jesus said to [the religious law-keepers], "The holy nation of
God is not coming in such a way that can be seen with the
eyes. It will not be said, 'See, here it is!' or, 'There it
is!' For the holy nation of God is in you."

LUKE 17:20–21

The Pharisees asked Jesus when the kingdom of God would come. They
did not realize that by Jesus coming, the kingdom of God was already
here. We enter the kingdom of God the moment we invite Jesus into our
hearts and commit to follow Him. Yes, we are waiting for Jesus to return
so that we can physically be with Him for eternity. And yes, there will
be a day when Jesus makes all things new and destroys all evil forever.
But we don't have to wait for heaven to be a part of God's kingdom. It's
already begun. Some people think we just have to endure this dark and
crazy world, and then we'll finally be happy. But Jesus wants us to start
living as part of His kingdom now. He wants us to experience abundant
and joyful lives right here (John 10:10). Jesus wants to fill us with His
light and love so that other people will want to be filled with His love too.

---

*Jesus, thank You for filling me with love and joy right
now. I'm so thankful we're friends and that I get to
experience Your love and joy for all eternity too.*

PRAY ALWAYS

Jesus told [His disciples] a picture-story to show that
men should always pray and not give up.
LUKE 18:1

Jesus told His followers another story about prayer. He told of a widow who kept going to see a judge about a matter. She was looking for the judge to right a wrong that had been done to her. The judge didn't care about God or people, so he sent her away. But she kept coming and coming until the judge was sick of her coming! He finally did what she asked because he wanted to stop her from bothering him. So if a wicked judge will grant a request because of someone's persistence, wouldn't God, who actually loves us, grant our requests when we are persistent? First Thessalonians 5:16–18 says, "Rejoice always, pray without ceasing, give thanks in all circumstances; for this is the will of God in Christ Jesus for you" (ESV). Jesus wants us to praise Him always—and pray always. That is God's will for us! People go around searching for God's plan for them their whole lives, but these verses say exactly what God's will is for us—to give thanks and pray! God's will for us is pretty simple after all.

Jesus, thank You for making Your will so simple for me. I want to praise You and talk to You for the rest of my life. Show me how to do this during good times and bad.

DOING THE IMPOSSIBLE

Jesus said, "God can do things men cannot do."
LUKE 18:27

Do you ever sit and think about just how great and powerful God is? Take a look at these verses:

- " 'For my thoughts are not your thoughts, neither are your ways my ways,' declares the LORD. 'As the heavens are higher than the earth, so are my ways higher than your ways and my thoughts than your thoughts' " (Isaiah 55:8–9 NIV).

- "Our Lord is great and very powerful. There is no limit to what he knows" (Psalm 147:5 ICB).

- "Do you realize where you are? You're in a cosmos star-flung with constellations by God, a world God wakes up each morning and puts to bed each night. God dips water from the ocean and gives the land a drink. GOD, God-revealed, does all this" (Amos 5:8 MSG).

God is the great creator of all things, and yet He cares deeply about everything that matters to you! If you have trouble believing that, read Psalm 139. God wants you to know how very loved you are. No matter what you are facing today, this year, or in the future, trust that God can do the impossible in your life. He is still the God of miracles.

Jesus, help me to believe that You care about everything that matters to me. I trust that You can still do the impossible today.

LOOKING AND SAVING

"The Son of Man came to look for and to save from
the punishment of sin those who are lost."

LUKE 19:10

Have you heard the children's song about Zacchaeus? "Zacchaeus was a
wee little man and a wee little man was he. He climbed up in a sycamore
tree for the Lord he wanted to see." You see, Zach was a short man, and he
couldn't see Jesus because of the big crowd. So, yep, he climbed a tree just
like the song says! Jesus saw him up in the tree and called for him to come
down. Jesus went to his house, and Zacchaeus chose to follow Jesus that
day. People were upset with Jesus for going to Zach's house. He was very
rich because he collected taxes and cheated people. But Jesus loved Zach,
and that love changed Zach's life. He immediately gave half his possessions
to the poor and promised to pay back four times the amount he cheated
anyone. Jesus said that He came to look for and save the lost. Jesus is still
looking for His lost ones and waiting for them to come to Him. It doesn't
matter if you have made very bad choices in the past. It doesn't matter if
you're rich or poor. It doesn't matter who your parents are. If you choose to
follow Jesus, Jesus will welcome you into His kingdom.

---

*Jesus, thank You for welcoming me into Your kingdom. Help me to
love others like You do, without worrying what others think of me.*

GIVING SACRIFICIALLY

[Jesus] said, "I tell you the truth, this poor woman has put in more than all of them. For they have put in a little of the money they had no need for. She is very poor and has put in all she had. She has put in what she needed for her own living."

LUKE 21:3–4

Jesus saw rich people putting money in the collection box at the temple. Then he saw a poor widow put in two small coins. Even though the rich men put in a bigger amount, Jesus said that the poor woman put in more. Why? Because she gave everything she had, trusting that God would take care of her. The rich men put in a lot, but it was money they didn't even need. It didn't cost them much of anything to give that money. The poor woman gave sacrificially. That means that she gave up something of great value to her as an act of worship to God. Have you ever worshipped God sacrificially? Maybe you volunteer at your church and help in ways that take up a lot of your time. Or maybe you've saved up a lot of money for your favorite video game but you know a family at church who is struggling to have enough to eat, so you decide to give them your money instead. Ask Jesus if He wants you to give something sacrificially. Talk about giving sacrificially as a family.

Jesus, I want to be a part of the ways You are blessing people in need around me. Please show me how I can help.

REMEMBERING

Then Jesus took bread and gave thanks and broke it in pieces.
He gave it to [his disciples], saying, "This is My body
which is given for you. Do this to remember Me."

LUKE 22:19

Does your church celebrate Communion? They might call it something different, like the Lord's Supper. Jesus asked us to remember Him in this way. We have bread to remember the body of Jesus. He calls Himself the "bread of life." We have wine or juice to remember the blood of Jesus that was shed for us on the cross. He gave up His life to save us. First Corinthians 11:29 says, "If you eat the bread or drink the cup without honoring the body of Christ, you are eating and drinking God's judgment upon yourself" (NLT). This is a serious time of worship where we are quiet and we pray. We thank Jesus for what He has done for us. Have you ever participated in Communion before? Ask your family to join you at home. You can find bread and juice and remember what Jesus has done as a family. Ask different family members to read scriptures about the Lord's Supper. Have a quiet time to ask Jesus to search your heart and show you anything that needs to be confessed and made right. Sing a worship song together.

*Jesus, we remember You as a family. Thank You for
Your sacrifice for us. We love You, Jesus.*

JESUS FORGIVES

Then Jesus said, "Father, forgive them.
They do not know what they are doing."
LUKE 23:34

If someone was trying to hurt you again and again, it would be really hard to forgive them. But as Jesus was being nailed to the cross, He asked God to forgive everyone who put Him there. The people didn't believe, and they didn't understand that they were killing God's Son—the only person who could save them. We find out later, in the book of Acts, that some of the religious leaders and priests became believers in Jesus. After Jesus was killed and came back to life, His disciples started sharing the Good News everywhere they went. People finally believed that Jesus was who He said He was—the Son of the living God. He is one with His Father. And He sent the Holy Spirit. As the old saying goes, "Hindsight is 20/20." That means that when you have the ability to look back on the past, you can see more clearly. After hearing of Jesus' life and resurrection, His persecutors were able to look back and see that everything Jesus said was true. And Jesus had already forgiven them.

Jesus, help me to be forgiving even when it's really hard. Do a work in my heart so that I can begin to love people the way You do.

TELLING THE TRUTH

As [the disciples] talked, Jesus Himself stood among them.
He said, "May you have peace." But they were afraid and full of fear.
They thought they saw a spirit. Jesus said to them, "Why are you
afraid? Why do you have doubts in your hearts? Look at My hands
and My feet. See! It is I, Myself! Touch Me and see for yourself.
A spirit does not have flesh and bones as I have." When Jesus
had said this, He showed them His hands and feet.

LUKE 24:36–40

After Jesus came back to life, He appeared to His followers. Even though Jesus' disciples had been with Him for a long time, listening to everything He had to say, they still could hardly believe that He had come back to life! Jesus showed them His scars from being nailed to the cross. It was really Him, in a new body that would never get old or die again. Jesus told the truth even when He knew His disciples wouldn't believe or understand. Have you ever been in a situation where telling the truth might make you look bad or silly? Jesus wants us to tell the truth. Lies come from the enemy, even the little lies that we think are unimportant. Lies cause people we love not to trust us, and that hurts us and them. Always tell the truth, like Jesus did.

Jesus, help me have the courage to tell the truth no matter what.

TELL WHAT YOU HAVE SEEN

"It must be preached that men must be sorry for their sins and turn from them. Then they will be forgiven. This must be preached in His name to all nations beginning in Jerusalem. You are to tell what you have seen."

LUKE 24:47–48

Have you seen Jesus answer your prayers before? Maybe you prayed for someone who was sick to get well. Maybe you prayed for help with a problem that seemed impossible to you. Maybe you prayed for your mom or dad to get a job after losing one. Take some time to write down what you've prayed for and how God has answered you. Jesus wants us to tell others about what we've seen Him do. He told the disciples to tell everyone about everything they saw and heard from Jesus. He wants us to share what He is doing in our lives too so that people will know that having a friendship with Jesus makes a difference. How has Jesus changed your life? Practice sharing your testimony, your personal story about what Jesus has done in your life. Write down how you first came to know Jesus and what He has been doing in your life since then. Your testimony about Jesus is powerful and important.

Jesus, thank You for all the amazing things You've done in my life. Use my testimony to bring other people to know You.

PRAYING AND GIVING THANKS

Jesus led [his disciples] out as far as Bethany. Then He lifted up His hands and prayed that good would come to them. And while He was praying that good would come to them, He went from them (and was taken up to heaven and they worshiped Him). Then they went back to Jerusalem with great joy. They spent all their time in the house of God honoring and giving thanks to God.

LUKE 24:50–53

Remember Jeremiah 29:11? This verse reminds us that God has good things in store for us. He wants good to come to us. He wants us to find Him and know Him personally. He wants us to know that we are never alone and that we always have access to the greatest power alive. That's the Good News! Psalm 31:19 says, "How wonderful are the good things you keep for those who honor you! Everyone knows how good you are, how securely you protect those who trust you" (GNT). Give thanks to Jesus for His goodness. Following Jesus is the most important decision you can ever make. Jesus will fill your life with adventure and love and peace if you let Him. This doesn't mean that life on earth will always be easy. What good adventure doesn't have a bit of risk in it? But Jesus always promises to be with you, and He gives you a special kind of peace that goes beyond natural human understanding (Philippians 4:7).

Jesus, I give You thanks for the adventure You have me on! I'm thankful for the great plans You have in store.

JESUS FROM THE BEGINNING

The Word (Christ) was in the beginning. The Word was with God. The Word was God. He was with God in the beginning. He made all things. Nothing was made without Him making it. Life began by Him. His Life was the Light for men. The Light shines in the darkness. The darkness has never been able to put out the Light.

JOHN 1:1–5

The book of John tells us so much about the life of Jesus. If you plan to read a whole book of the Bible, the book of John is a great one to start with. John was one of Jesus' twelve disciples, so he was there to see Jesus' mighty works firsthand. John begins by telling us that Jesus has always existed, even before He was born as a human on earth! Can anyone else say that? Jesus was completely God and completely man. Jesus is the image of the invisible God (Colossians 1:15) who made the whole world. And Colossians 2:9 tells us, "In Christ lives all the fullness of God in a human body" (NLT). When you put your trust in Jesus, you are putting your faith in the one true God who was and is and is to come (Revelation 1:8).

Jesus, I might not be able to comprehend everything about You, but I do put my faith and trust in You.

CHILDREN OF GOD

*[Jesus] gave the right and the power to become children
of God to those who received Him. He gave this
to those who put their trust in His name.*

JOHN 1:12

When you receive Jesus as your Savior, you become a child of God. John 1:13 tells us that you become "born of God." Can you believe it? When you were born as a baby, you came alive physically. When you were "born of God," you came alive spiritually. The day you accepted Jesus as your Savior was your spiritual birthday. It's something fun and important to celebrate! If you know when you asked Jesus into your heart, write down the day and plan a celebration. If you don't know the exact day, ask your family to help you estimate so you have a close idea. Becoming a child of God comes with a huge inheritance! (An inheritance is something—often of value—that is passed down in families.) First Peter 1:4 tells us that "we have a priceless inheritance—an inheritance that is kept in heaven for you, pure and undefiled, beyond the reach of change and decay" (NLT). We don't know what all this includes, but we do know that Jesus is the Most High King, and we are His brothers and sisters, adopted into God's family. Our inheritance will be beyond our imagination.

---

*Jesus, I'm so thankful I gave my life to You and became a child
of God! Thank You for providing an inheritance
for me that will never go away.*

GOD BECAME ONE OF US

Christ became human flesh and lived among us. We saw His shining-greatness. This greatness is given only to a much-loved Son from His Father. He was full of loving-favor and truth.

JOHN 1:14

Jesus came to earth and became a man so that we could know Him completely. He placed His Spirit in our hearts. Now there is no longer any separation between God and humans, unless we choose to put it there. Jesus came to love us and show us the truth. Many people think God is like a grumpy old man who is only out to spoil their fun. Jesus showed us that that couldn't be further from the truth. Philippians 2:6–8 tells us a bit more about this: "Christ himself was like God in everything. He was equal with God. But he did not think that being equal with God was something to be held on to. He gave up his place with God and made himself nothing. He was born as a man and became like a servant. And when he was living as a man, he humbled himself and was fully obedient to God. He obeyed even when that caused his death—death on a cross" (ICB). Jesus gave up His place in heaven to come and save us!

Jesus, I'm so thankful You chose to enter our world so that we can enter Yours. Help me live each day with a thankful heart.

YOU CAN TRUST HIM

[Changing water into wine] was the first powerful work Jesus did.
It was done in Cana of Galilee where He showed His power.
His followers put their trust in Him.

JOHN 2:11

Jesus was at a wedding when they ran out of wine to drink. Weddings in Bible times were often weeklong events. A lot of planning had to go into how much food and drink would be needed to satisfy all the guests. Running out of food or drink at such an event would be humiliating. Jesus told the servants to fill large jars with water. Then He miraculously turned the water into the best wine. Jesus didn't do this to draw attention to Himself. He likely felt compassion for the bride and groom and didn't want them to suffer humiliation on their special day. The book of John tells us that this was Jesus' first miraculous sign. He had recently asked disciples to follow Him, but they hadn't yet realized who Jesus was or the power He had. When they saw the power Jesus had over nature to turn water into wine, they believed in Him. Jesus is a personal Savior. He went to parties and loved people individually. The disciples decided they could put their trust in a good friend like that. How about you?

Jesus, I am thankful that You are such a good friend—the very best! I'm happy that You take time to get to know me and that You want the best for me. I trust You, Jesus!

LIFE THAT LASTS FOREVER

"For God so loved the world that He gave His only Son.
Whoever puts his trust in God's Son will not be lost but will
have life that lasts forever. For God did not send His Son into
the world to say it is guilty. He sent His Son so the world
might be saved from the punishment of sin by Him."

JOHN 3:16–17

If you decide to memorize just one verse in the Bible, it should probably be John 3:16, the most well-known verse in the Bible. It sums up the entire Gospel. It's the Good News! It's also a great verse to share with people who want to know more about Jesus. John 3:17 is important too. Jesus didn't come to condemn us, He came to save us. He is our Savior. The ancient theologian Augustine said that "God loves each of us as if there were only one of us." And when we believe and receive Christ as our Lord and Savior, we are guaranteed a life that lasts forever. Making Jesus Lord of our lives means that we choose to let Him lead us throughout our lives. We follow His Word and His ways.

Jesus, You've offered me a life that lasts forever, and I accept.
I'm so blessed that You chose me to be Your child.
Please lead me in Your truth and in Your ways.

A WELL OF LIFE

"Whoever drinks the water that I [Jesus] will give him will never
be thirsty. The water that I will give him will become in
him a well of life that lasts forever."

JOHN 4:14

Jesus was traveling and sat down by a well to rest. A Samaritan woman
came to get water. Jews hated Samaritans and would not be seen talking
to them, especially to women. Jesus wanted all people to receive His
living water, the power of the Holy Spirit that flows from Him. He did
not show prejudice to any people groups, and He treated women and
children with kindness and respect. This was often unheard of in Bible
times. But Jesus struck up a conversation with the Samaritan woman.
He showed her love and respect even though she lived a sinful life. He
used the opportunity to speak to her of everlasting life. Isaiah 58:11 tells
us this: "The Lord will always lead you. He will satisfy your needs in
dry lands. He will give strength to your bones. You will be like a garden
that has much water. You will be like a spring that never runs dry" (ICB).
When we put our trust in Jesus, He will fill us with living water that
bubbles up and spills over onto everyone around us!

Jesus, I ask that You continually fill me with Your living water.
Let it spill out and bless everyone around me so
that they will come to know You too.

THE KIND OF WORSHIPER GOD WANTS

"The time is coming, yes, it is here now, when the true worshipers will worship the Father in spirit and in truth. The Father wants that kind of worshipers."

JOHN 4:23

Worshipping God in spirit means that we are worshipping Him from our hearts wherever we are. We don't have to go to a church or be with other people to worship God in spirit. We can do it right from our own rooms. *The Message* helps us understand what this verse means: "It's who you are and the way you live that count before God. Your worship must engage your spirit in the pursuit of truth. That's the kind of people the Father is out looking for: those who are simply and honestly themselves before him in their worship. God is sheer being itself—Spirit. Those who worship him must do it out of their very being, their spirits, their true selves, in adoration" (John 4:23–24). When we worship God in truth, it means that we're honestly being ourselves before God. We aren't hiding anything or pretending to be something we're not. These are the kind of worshippers Jesus wants us to be.

Jesus, I want to worship You in a way that makes You happy. Help me to be honest and true when I come to You. Thank You that I can come to You from anywhere! Even from my own bed!

DEATH TO LIFE

"For sure, I tell you, anyone who hears My Word and puts his trust in Him Who sent Me has life that lasts forever. He will not be guilty. He has already passed from death into life."

JOHN 5:24

Eternal life is not something you have to wait for. The moment you accept Jesus as your Savior, you pass from death to life. You are guaranteed a life that lasts forever. Remember the stories in the Bible about Jesus raising people to life? Physical death on this earth is not the end! The promises of Jesus are more powerful than death. Acts 2:24 tells us, "God raised him from the dead, freeing him from the agony of death, because it was impossible for death to keep its hold on him" (NIV). And we are given that same promise. Death does not have a hold on us anymore. Jesus completely conquered and destroyed death forever. Romans 6:23 confirms this promise: "The wages of sin is death, but the free gift of God is eternal life in Christ Jesus our Lord" (ESV). Remember, Jesus took all our sin and punishment when He sacrificed His life for us. First Corinthians 1:2 says we are sanctified, which means we are declared holy. God looks at us as clean and holy because of Jesus. What a life!

Jesus, I praise and thank You for all You've done for me! Thank You that death is not the end. I'm so thankful that I have eternal life!

FULL WITH LIFE

Jesus said to [the crowd], "For sure, I tell you, you are not looking
for Me because of the powerful works. You are looking for Me
because you ate bread and were filled. Do not work for food
that does not last. Work for food that lasts forever. The Son
of Man will give you that kind of food. God the
Father has shown He will do this."

JOHN 6:26–27

The crowds were looking for Jesus again because they were hungry. They saw Him multiply the loaves and fishes and feed thousands. Jesus had given them all a free meal. They knew He could do it again if He wanted to. They weren't necessarily coming to hear what Jesus had to say. They wanted something for nothing. But Jesus called them out on it. He told them not to come and listen to Him to fill their stomachs with food, but to come listen so that their hearts would be filled with life. Jesus was talking about "spiritual food." Just as we need to eat every day to live and grow, we need to have Jesus and His Word in us every day so that we can live and grow spiritually. Reading devotional books like this one, praying to Jesus, and reading God's Word every day are just some of the ways you can grow spiritually. Think about other ways you can grow in your relationship with Jesus and write them down.

---

*Jesus, thank You for my daily food so that I'm not hungry.
I ask that You would fill me up with Your life and love too.*

THE BREAD OF LIFE

Jesus said to [the crowd], "I am the Bread of Life. He who comes to Me will never be hungry. He who puts his trust in Me will never be thirsty."

JOHN 6:35

Have you ever made homemade bread? It smells yummy as it's baking and when it's cooling, fresh from the oven. It's so much easier to go out and buy bread from the store, but you may be surprised at how much you like homemade bread if you give it a try. Back in Bible times, each family had to make their own bread. Bread was often their main food, and it could take two or three hours just to make enough bread for each family for one day. Jesus said that He is our Bread of Life. Just as the people of the Bible had to make fresh bread every day for their physical nourishment, we need to come to Jesus every day for our spiritual nourishment. Without receiving spiritual food from Jesus, we cannot grow in our faith. Ask your parents if they will help you gather the ingredients to make your own homemade bread. As you're preparing and baking, ask Jesus to fill your heart with His truth and love. Now go share the Bread of Life, and your homemade bread, with your family and friends.

Jesus, thank You for meeting my daily needs for physical food and spiritual food. Help me to always be willing to share both with my friends and neighbors.

WHEN YOU COME TO JESUS

"All whom My Father has given to Me will come to Me.
I will never turn away anyone who comes to Me."

JOHN 6:37

When You come to Jesus for the first time or the millionth time, you can be sure that His arms are open. He runs to meet you—even if you've messed up. Jesus says He will never turn anyone away who comes to Him. Romans 2:4 tells us some very special things about God: "Don't you see how wonderfully kind, tolerant, and patient God is with you? Does this mean nothing to you? Can't you see that his kindness is intended to turn you from your sin?" (NLT). It's the kindness of God that leads us to Jesus, to have our sins forgiven. If you've made a big mistake, the best thing you can do is to go straight to Jesus and talk to Him about it. You can do this from your school, your backyard, your bedroom—anywhere! Jesus promises that He will not turn you away. He will not make you feel shame or make you feel bad about yourself. He will tell you He loves you and show you ways that you can change.

Jesus, thank You for your loving-kindness to me. When I make mistakes, remind me that You love me and that You'll never turn me away. You are my best friend and my wise counselor.

DECISIONS

Then Jesus said to the twelve followers, "Will you leave Me also?"
Simon Peter said to Him, "Lord, who else can we go to?
You have words that give life that lasts forever."

JOHN 6:67–68

You're going to have to make a lot of important choices as you grow up. Will you stay strong in your faith? What will you do with your life? Will you give in to pressure from friends to make choices that you know are wrong? Growing up and making decisions can be a scary thing. Isaiah 30:21 gives us great encouragement! "If you go the wrong way—to the right or to the left—you will hear a voice behind you. It will say, 'This is the right way. You should go this way' " (ICB). The disciples had big decisions to make too. Would they keep the faith or cave to the crowd? Jesus gives us the Holy Spirit to help us make these important decisions. You can be sure that Jesus will lead you if you're listening for His voice. This may not be a voice you hear out loud; it's more like a warning system inside your head and your heart. Ask Jesus to help you know when He's talking to you. Jesus loves to confirm what He is saying to you through His words in the Bible, through other believers, and even through worship music.

---

*Jesus, help me get better at hearing Your voice. I need Your
help making decisions. Thank You for promising
to show me the right way!*

HEALTHY TREE

"The Holy Writings say that rivers of living water will flow
from the heart of the one who puts his trust in Me."

JOHN 7:38

Isn't it cool to think that you have living water from Jesus flowing through you? What do you think Jesus wants to do with that water? Psalm 1:3 tells us more about this: "That person is like a tree planted by streams of water, which yields its fruit in season and whose leaf does not wither—whatever they do prospers" (NIV). When you live your life for Jesus and allow Him to fill you with His living water, you become like a healthy tree that is planted by a stream and produces a lot of fruit. Trees that produce a lot of fruit can feed and bring joy to a lot of people. So can you! As you grow in your faith, Jesus will fill you with more and more living water to produce more and more fruit. Of course you won't start growing apples on your body. These are fruit of the Spirit like love, joy, peace, and patience (Galatians 5:22–23). We'll talk more about those soon. For now, ask Jesus to continue to fill you with His living water, and be on the lookout for fruit!

---

*Jesus, I'm excited and thankful that You're filling me
with living water! Help me grow fruit that will
bless my family and friends with Your love.*

THE LIGHT OF LIFE

Jesus spoke to all the people, saying, "I am the Light of
the world. Anyone who follows Me will not walk in
darkness. He will have the Light of Life."

JOHN 8:12

The world we live in today is kind of dark. People are always fighting
with one another. Some countries hate each other and start wars. People
spend most of their time with a screen in their face instead of living real
life. The enemy loves to keep people distracted and busy. When evil gets
ahold of a person, they make really bad choices. That's why the light of
Jesus is so important in our world today! And you have it! If you follow
Jesus, He gives you His light so that you don't have to walk in darkness.
You don't have to follow the crowd into dark places. You can be a leader
with a bright light that people will want to follow. When they see a light
in the darkness, people want that. They'll want to know what causes you
to be joyful and loving. They'll want to know where that light and love
come from. It's your job as a follower of Jesus to let that light shine as
brightly as possible!

---

*Jesus, please keep my light shining as bright as possible.
Thank You for keeping me out of the darkness. Help me
to be a bright leader in a distracted and dark world.*

OBEYING JESUS

As Jesus said these things, many people put their trust in Him.
He said to the Jews who believed, "If you keep and obey
My Word, then you are My followers for sure."

JOHN 8:30–31

Jesus wants us to obey Him. Obedience is how we show that we love Him. When we obey our parents, we show that we love and trust them. It's the same with Jesus! How do we know if we're obeying Jesus? We check in His Word, the Bible. He gives us some important rules that you can look up in Exodus 20:1–17. These are called the Ten Commandments, and they include rules like putting God first, obeying your parents, and not lying or stealing. Knowing these rules and what they mean is vital, so check them out with your parents. Ephesians 4:32 gives us some more important rules to obey: "Be kind and loving to each other. Forgive each other just as God forgave you in Christ" (ICB). The Christian life is not all about rules, though. Jesus gives us these rules or boundaries so that we can be free! Following these boundaries that Jesus has set up for us will give us the best outcome in life and keep us from a lot of negative consequences. Jesus wants what is best for us! Just like good parents do.

Jesus, I want to obey You because I love You. Thank You for giving me good boundaries so that I can live a full and joyful life. I trust You, Jesus, and I believe You want what is best for me.

THE ENEMY

"The devil has nothing to do with the truth. There is no truth
in him. It is expected of the devil to lie, for he is
a liar and the father of lies."

JOHN 8:44

Jesus tells us that we have an enemy that is out to kill, steal from, and
destroy us (John 10:10). That's a pretty scary thing to think about. But
here's the deal: Jesus is astronomically more powerful than the devil, and so
we don't give him that much attention. God and Satan are not equals. Not
even close. Not even on the same playing field. Satan is a liar, so he might
try and get you to believe that he is way more powerful than he is. When
you're scared or facing something that comes from the enemy, call out to
Jesus and let Him handle it. Don't focus on your fears; focus on Jesus.

Here's what you need to know about the enemy:

- Satan is real (1 Peter 5:8).
- He is a liar (John 8:44) and sometimes pretends to be good
  (2 Corinthians 11:14).
- He tries to lead us away from Jesus (2 Corinthians 11:3).
- He is defeated (1 John 3:8).
- Jesus' power in you is greater than the enemy's power
  (1 John 4:4).
- You are safe from the devil when you trust in Jesus (James 4:7).

---

*Jesus, thank You for Your protection from the enemy.
I know that You are more powerful than any tricks
he might try to play on me. I am safe with You.*

LISTENING TO HIS WORD

"Whoever is born of God listens to God's Word."
JOHN 8:47

Here are some great verses to know about God's Word:

- "Your word is a lamp for my feet, a light on my path. . . .
  The unfolding of your words gives light; it gives
  understanding to the simple." (Psalm 119:105, 130 NIV)

- "The precepts of the Lord are right, giving joy to the
  heart. The commands of the Lord are radiant, giving light
  to the eyes." (Psalm 19:8 NIV)

God's Word is a lamp for our feet. Reading and knowing God's Word provides us with light so our feet know the next steps to take. We are to obey Jesus step by step and moment by moment. Even when we don't understand what He's doing. Even when obedience doesn't make any sense. Jesus gives us boundaries and guidance (rules) for a reason. He has purpose in everything He does and in everything He asks us to do. Jesus promises that all things work together for our good and for His glory (Romans 8:28)! But if Jesus shared all the details with us up front, we would most likely run the other way. There are some life lessons we all have to learn that aren't easy and fun. But Jesus lights up our path just enough so that we can see how to obey Him—step by step and moment by moment.

---

*Jesus, I don't always understand everything You're doing
in my life, but I trust You. Help me to get into Your
Word and know You better in each moment.*

A GREAT, FULL LIFE

"The robber comes only to steal and to kill and to destroy.
I [Jesus] came so they might have life, a great full life."
JOHN 10:10

King Solomon wrote the book of Ecclesiastes to remind us that life is meaningless unless we are following God. Solomon had wealth and power and whatever He wanted, but He admitted that it was all worth nothing because He chose to ignore God for many years. He wrote Ecclesiastes as he was looking back on his life. You may wish for lots of money and want a lot of things you don't have, but take a look at all that Solomon had to say. In Ecclesiastes 3:12–13 he said, "I know that there is nothing better for people than to be happy and to do good while they live. That each of them may eat and drink, and find satisfaction in all their toil—this is the gift of God" (NIV). God wants us to enjoy life—but *with* Him and not apart from Him. Some people think that it's more fun to ignore God and do whatever they want, but Solomon knew this is not true. John 10:10 tells us that Jesus came so that we can have abundant life—a good and joyful life—here and for all eternity!

Jesus, remind me that You want me to live a joyful life with You, not apart from You. You are the One who brings true joy to my life. I know that every good gift comes from You [James 1:17].

OUR SHEPHERD

"I am the Good Shepherd. The Good Shepherd
gives His life for the sheep."
JOHN 10:11

To love Jesus, you have to know and understand certain things about Him. He said in John 10:27–30, "My sheep listen to my voice; I know them, and they follow me. I give them eternal life, and they shall never perish; no one can snatch them out of my hand. My Father, who has given them to me, is greater than all; no one can snatch them out of my Father's hand. I and the Father are one" (NIV). We don't see shepherds too much in our culture, but back in Bible times, shepherds were common. Many of the great heroes of the Bible were shepherds, including Moses and David. A good and gentle shepherd would love and care for his sheep with compassion and kindness. He needed the sheep to listen to him so they could travel to the best places for food. When the shepherd walked ahead of them, they followed him because they knew his voice. Jesus calls us His sheep, and He lovingly cares for each of us! Today's verse reminds us that our shepherd even gave His very life for us! When we get to know His voice, we can be sure we're following someone we can trust.

Jesus, You are my loving Shepherd. I follow You because I trust You
and know that I can count on You to lead me to the right places.

GIVING HIS LIFE

"No one takes my life from Me. I give it by Myself. I have the
right and the power to take it back again. My Father
has given Me this right and power."

JOHN 10:18

A victim is a person who suffers from something bad done to them.
Someone who has a "victim mentality" will often say things like "poor
me" and act as if everyone else is responsible for what happens to them.
Jesus said that He wasn't a victim. While people did do a lot of bad things
to Him, He allowed them to do so. He could have stopped them at any
moment because He is the creator of the universe. But He allowed all
the bad things to happen to fulfill God's purpose and to save us from
our sins. There was no other way to save us and make us right with God.
Matthew 20:28 tells us that Jesus gave His life for our ransom. *Ransom*
in this verse means to release from punishment of sin. Jesus paid our
ransom, once and for all. Romans 6:23 explains, "The payment for sin is
death. But God gives us the free gift of life forever in Christ Jesus our
Lord" (ICB). We've been given the free gift of life forever. Stop and think
about that. Thank Jesus for this astounding gift every day.

*Jesus, I'm so thankful that You paid my ransom. I can't
imagine the pain You went through on purpose for me.
Help me live my life to say thanks to You!*

JESUS RAISES THE DEAD

Jesus said to [Martha], "I am the One Who raises the dead and gives them life. Anyone who puts his trust in Me will live again, even if he dies. Anyone who lives and has put his trust in Me will never die. Do you believe this?"

JOHN 11:25–26

Jesus had some friends named Mary, Martha, and Lazarus. They were sisters and brother. Jesus spent time with them and loved them. Lazarus got sick. Mary and Martha tried to take good care of him, but he kept getting sicker and sicker. They sent for Jesus to come, but Jesus didn't g to them right away. He told them that what was about to happen would show people how awesome God really is. Jesus waited a couple of days to go and see them. But during those days, Lazarus died. Martha was upset at Jesus for not coming right away. But she didn't really know how powerful Jesus was yet, even though He was her friend. She didn't understand that Jesus had all power over life and death. Mary was upset too. Jesus had compassion for both of them and cried along with them. Jesus went to the tomb where Lazarus was buried and called, "Lazarus, come out!" (John 11:43). So, of course he did! Jesus brought him back to life. Many people saw the glory of God that day and put their faith in Jesus.

Thank You, Jesus, for having complete power over life and death!

NO MORE DARKNESS

"I came to the world to be a Light. Anyone who puts
his trust in Me will not be in darkness."

JOHN 12:46

Have you ever been afraid of the dark? Even some grown-ups are afraid of the dark. Being in a room that is all dark, especially a room you've never been in before, can be a little scary. Dark basements can be really frightening. But what happens when you flip the light switch? The darkness goes away and the room isn't so scary anymore. It's full of light now. Jesus came to be a light in the darkness. When we shine His light on anything, the darkness goes away. When you allow Jesus to light up your heart, the darkness of sin goes away too. Tonight, as a family, wait till it's dark outside and then turn off all the lights in your house. Hold your mom's or dad's hand as you stand in the darkness for a few minutes. Then turn the lights back on and thank Jesus that you have electricity! Did it help to be holding someone's hand in the dark? Of course it did. It's not so scary in the dark when we know we're not alone. Jesus is the Light that's with you always. You are never alone. When life on this earth seems extra dark, remember that Jesus is holding on to you.

Jesus, I'm relieved and thankful that I am never alone.
You are always with me.

LOVE EACH OTHER

"I give you a new Law. You are to love each other. You must love
each other as I have loved you. If you love each other,
all men will know you are My followers."

JOHN 13:34–35

Jesus gave His disciples a new command: "Love each other." Loving
each other wasn't a new law. God told the Hebrew people in the Old
Testament to love each other too. But loving like Jesus was definitely
new. No one had ever loved them like Jesus did. That's what He was
asking His disciples to do. And that's what He's asking us to do too. He
says that other people will know we follow Jesus because we show love.
Can you imagine treating everyone you meet like they were Jesus? And
loving them like they were Jesus? What would it be like to treat your
brother or sister like they were Jesus instead of treating them like an
annoying family member who sometimes gets on your nerves? Do you
think that would change your family? You bet it would! Why not give it
a try? Ask Jesus for help to treat other people like they are Jesus Himself.
Try it at school, at home, in the grocery store—anywhere you go. You
can start changing the world by loving people the way Jesus wants us to.

---

*Jesus, I'm not sure I'll be able to love people like You do.
It seems really hard! Especially with my brother
and sister! Can You please help?*

DON'T BE TROUBLED

"Do not let your heart be troubled. You have put your
trust in God, put your trust in Me also."

JOHN 14:1

This is a great verse to memorize for when you are scared or worried
about something. Jesus wants you to trust Him and not be afraid. He
is good, and He loves you very much. Check out Psalm 18:16–19: "He
reached down from heaven and rescued me; he drew me out of deep
waters. He rescued me from my powerful enemies, from those who hated
me and were too strong for me. They attacked me at a moment when
I was in distress, but the LORD supported me. He led me to a place of
safety; he rescued me because he delights in me" (NLT). These are true
words that you can count on. "Deep water" in this verse means more
than just rescuing you from a lake or an ocean. Deep water can also mean
any hard times you may be having. Maybe there are some mean kids at
school. Maybe you have a sick friend or family member. Maybe your dog
passed away. Jesus cares about all of that, and He wants to support you.
The Bible says that He will lead you to a place of safety. He can bring
people and supplies to meet any need you have. Just talk to Him about it.
Jesus loves to show you what He can do.

Jesus, I trust that You can and will rescue me from any troubles.

MY FATHER'S HOUSE

"There are many rooms in My Father's house. If it were not so,
I would have told you. I am going away to make a place for you.
After I go and make a place for you, I will come back and
take you with Me. Then you may be where I am."

JOHN 14:2–3

Think about the house you live in. How many bedrooms does it have? If you invited all your friends from school or church to come over and spend the night, would they fit? If your house was super big, maybe! But what if you invited everyone from school and church to come over? Would they all fit? Probably not. God's house is not like our house. We don't know much about what eternity will be like because the Bible doesn't give us a ton of details. But we do know this:

- There will be no tears or death in heaven (Revelation 21:4).

- The walls will be made of precious stones, and the streets paved with gold (Revelation 21:18–21).

- There will be no sun or moon because the glory of God will be the light (Revelation 21:23).

- There will be plenty of space for everyone who loves Jesus (John 14:2).

Jesus has plenty of room in His house for everyone who loves and trusts Him, and He is preparing a special place just for you!

---

*Jesus, I'm so excited to have a reservation in Your house
for all of eternity! Thanks for making a place for me.*

THE WAY, THE TRUTH, AND THE LIFE

Jesus said, "I am the Way and the Truth and the Life.
No one can go to the Father except by Me."
JOHN 14:6

There are a lot of religions in this world, but Jesus is the only way to God. You will hear about all kinds of religions as you grow older. Many of them might sound pretty good. But unless someone confesses Jesus Christ as Lord and commits to follow Him, that person cannot go to be with God. No one gets to God the Father unless they go through Jesus. Acts 4:12 also tells us, "Salvation is found in no one else, for there is no other name under heaven given to mankind by which we must be saved" (NIV). Remember that Jesus is all the fullness of God in human form (Colossians 2:9), and He is the image of the invisible God (Colossians 1:15). Jesus is how we can see God (John 1:18). God Himself came down to find you through Jesus. He is the Way, the Truth, and the Life.

---

*Jesus, I believe that You are the One true God. I will follow
You because You are the only Way and the Truth.
Through You alone, I find eternal life.*

OBEDIENCE

"If you love Me, you will do what I say."
JOHN 14:15

We show our love for God by loving and obeying Him and by loving others. When we have faith in Jesus, we follow Him because we trust His heart for us. He wants the very best for us just as good parents want what is best for their children—only even more so because God is perfect! Psalm 9:10 tells us, "Those who know your name trust in you, for you, O LORD, do not abandon those who search for you" (NLT). Kids (and adults too) who get to know the real Jesus of the Bible, know that they can trust Him. Jesus never leaves us and is always willing to welcome anyone who comes to Him. So we have faith that Jesus will lead us in the right direction. We may not know exactly where Jesus is leading us, but we trust Him to lovingly show us where He wants us to go. We can obey someone we trust. Do you have a teacher at church or school who is kind and loving? You want to do what they say because you trust them. It's the same with our loving God.

Jesus, I don't know where You'll take me on this life adventure,
but I trust Your heart for me. I choose to obey You!

OUR HELPER

"Then I will ask My Father and He will give you another
Helper. He will be with you forever. He is the Spirit of Truth.
The world cannot receive Him. It does not see Him or know Him.
You know Him because He lives with you and will be in you."

JOHN 14:16–17

God has put His very own Spirit in our hearts—the Holy Spirit, our
Helper! Second Corinthians 1:21–22 says, "It is God who makes both us
and you stand firm in Christ. He anointed us, set his seal of ownership
on us, and put his Spirit in our hearts as a deposit, guaranteeing what is
to come" (NIV). How powerful! He makes us stand firm in Christ. We
are His. We have a guarantee of what is to come! John 14:26 tells us,
"The Helper is the Holy Spirit. The Father will send Him in My place.
He will teach you everything and help you remember everything I have
told you." Do you need help with something? Does something seem too
big for you to handle? Come before Jesus in the quietness of your heart
and talk to Him. Tell Him your thoughts, your wants, and your needs.
Tell Him if you're feeling bad about something or if you need an answer
about something that's bothering You. Jesus is listening, and He is always
available. His Spirit will teach you everything you need to know.

---

*Jesus, thank You for sending Your Spirit inside
me to be my Teacher and Helper.*

JESUS IN OUR HEARTS

"In a little while the world will see Me no more. You will see
Me. Because I live, you will live also. When that day comes,
you will know that I am in My Father. You will know
that you are in Me. You will know that I am in you."

JOHN 14:19–20

Soon we will be able to see Jesus as He really is. Can you imagine actually
seeing Jesus face-to-face for the first time? First John 3:2–3 says, "Dear
friends, we are already God's children, but he has not yet shown us what
we will be like when Christ appears. But we do know that we will be
like him, for we will see him as he really is. And all who have this eager
expectation will keep themselves pure, just as he is pure" (NLT). While
we wait for Jesus to return, God wants us to be pure, like He is. But
remember, we can't do this on our own. The Bible says that if you are a
follower of Jesus, you are being transformed into His likeness day by day
(2 Corinthians 3:17–18). His Spirit invades your life and changes you...
keeping you pure for what is to come.

---

*Jesus, thank You for Your Spirit who is always at work in my
heart. Thank You that I don't have to be afraid or worried that
I have to live a pure life all on my own. I'm Yours, Jesus!*

THE PEACE OF JESUS

"Peace I leave with you. My peace I give to you. I do not give peace to you as the world gives. Do not let your hearts be troubled or afraid."

JOHN 14:27

Think about a peaceful place. What does it look like? Maybe somewhere by an ocean with a light breeze? Maybe a grassy field with butterflies? Peaceful places can be great to relax in. But having peace in your heart doesn't mean that everything is perfect and nothing is going wrong in your life. That idea is not what the Bible teaches. Jesus gives us true peace. When you experience the true peace that comes only from Him, you experience a deep knowing that no matter what happens to you or what is going wrong in your life, Jesus is still in control. This type of peace is the peace that goes beyond what our human minds can understand. This verse tells us that Jesus doesn't give to us as the world gives to us. When we receive something from someone here on earth, these gifts usually don't last for very long. The gift of peace from Jesus is eternal and available to all of us who call Him our Savior. That means that you don't have to be afraid. Your heart can rest as you trust Jesus to take care of you.

Dear Jesus, thank You for giving me Your peace that is beyond what I can understand. Help me not to be afraid in times of trouble, but to remember that You are always with me.

THE VINE

"I am the Vine and you are the branches. Get your life
from Me. Then I will live in you and you will give
much fruit. You can do nothing without Me."

JOHN 15:5

Do you like to eat grapes? The next time you have grapes in your refrigerator, take them out and look at them. How many grapes are still attached to the vine? They are the yummy, firm, fresh grapes. Do you see any that have fallen off the vine to the bottom of the package or container? They are usually squishy and gross. You have to throw those ones away. This tells us a lot about our relationship with Jesus. Jesus is the Vine. When we are living close to Him by talking to Him, worshipping Him, and reading His Word—we are attached to Him. Our hearts are full of Jesus, and we are fresh and inviting. But when we fall away from Jesus the Vine, we can get grumpy and selfish just like a grape that's squishy and gross. What kind of fruit do you want to be? Squishy and gross or fresh and inviting? Stay close to Jesus, and He will give you abundant life. Isn't it cool that Jesus uses fruit to teach us?

*Jesus, I want to be a fresh fruit that's connected to the
Vine. I want to stay close to You and learn from You.
Thank You for teaching me in ways I can understand.*

STAY IN THE LOVE OF JESUS

"I have loved you just as My Father has loved Me. Stay in My love. If you obey My teaching, you will live in My love. In this way, I have obeyed My Father's teaching and live in His love. I have told you these things so My joy may be in you and your joy may be full."

JOHN 15:9–11

In John 15 Jesus tells us how we can show our love for God: by obeying His commands. What are His commands? To love God and love others. Jesus tells us that everything else depends on those two things (Matthew 22:36–40). Jesus wants us to know that love is the most important thing. First Corinthians 13 says that we are nothing without love. Do you remember when you first felt the love of Jesus? Picture it in your mind. How did you feel? What did you do? The Bible warns us not to forget our first love, Jesus. Revelation 2:4–5 says, "You have left the love you had in the beginning. So remember where you were before you fell. Change your hearts and do what you did at first" (ICB). Staying in Jesus' love means seeking Him first and talking to Him about everything. If you feel far from Jesus, tell Him you are sorry for forgetting Him. Ask Him to help You put Him first in Your life.

Jesus, I'm sorry when I don't put You first in my life.
Please change my heart to want to be with You more.

UNFAILING LOVE

"This is what I tell you to do: Love each other just as I have
loved you. No one can have greater love than
to give his life for his friends."

JOHN 15:12–13

God is God, and He could have chosen a million different ways to save us, but He chose to show us the true meaning of love. You can't show any more love for someone than to give up your life for them. Giving up your life for someone else is true, unselfish love. It's hard to imagine that kind of love. God chose to send His Son into the world to live just like us, to become our Friend, and to eventually lay down His life and die on the cross to show how much He actually loves us. This wasn't an accident. He knew the cost. Jesus knew it would hurt. He knew He would suffer. He knew He would be betrayed by some of the people closest to Him. But He went to the cross anyway so that we could be made right with God—once and for all. His love—a love that never fails or lets us down— is available to all of us who seek Him! Ask Jesus to fill you with His love. Then share it with others!

---

*Jesus, Your unfailing love for me is something I'll always
be trying to figure out. Thank You for coming to
make me right with You. I love You, Jesus!*

FRIENDS WITH JESUS

"You are My friends if you do what I tell you. I do not call you
servants that I own anymore. A servant does not know what
his owner is doing. I call you friends, because I have told
you everything I have heard from My Father."

JOHN 15:14–15

Through all that Jesus did for us on the cross, He made us children of God! But we're not just God's children; Jesus actually calls us His friends! Have you ever thought about what being a friend of God means? When you look for a friend, you want someone who is kind, trustworthy, and willing to listen. Jesus wants to have that very same kind of relationship with you. He wants you to know that you are never *ever* alone! He wants you to live a life of confidence and joy, knowing that God is working everything out for your good and His glory—even the bad things that happen during this life. Romans 5:2 tells us, "Because of our faith, Christ has brought us into this place of undeserved privilege where we now stand, and we confidently and joyfully look forward to sharing God's glory" (NLT). When trouble comes your way, you can look at it with peace, knowing that your very best Friend has it covered.

Jesus, how awesome that You call me Your friend!
That makes me confident that I can go
through life with joy in my heart!

NO ONE CAN TAKE YOUR JOY

"You are sad now. I will see you again and then your hearts
will be full of joy. No one can take your joy from you."

JOHN 16:22

You have a choice every day when you wake up. You can choose to be
thankful for a new day and look at it with joy and hopeful expectation,
or you can choose to let the day get ahead of you and spend the rest of
the day trying to catch up. The second choice happens a lot if we aren't
careful. And instead of looking at each moment as a gift, we are full
of stress and worry. Ask Jesus to help you see each new day as a gift.
As you wake up, ask Him to go before you and remind you that His
Spirit is always with you. Then, even if you're headed to a dreaded dentist
appointment, you'll be able to see the little blessings that God sends your
way as you look for Him. Romans 15:13 is a prayer that can help: "May
the God of hope fill you with all joy and peace as you trust in him, so
that you may overflow with hope by the power of the Holy Spirit" (NIV).

---

*Jesus, please help me choose to see each day and each moment
as a gift. Change my attitude to be like Yours. Fill me
with joy and hope that overflows.*

ASK AND RECEIVE

"Until now you have not asked for anything in My name.
Ask and you will receive. Then your joy will be full."
JOHN 16:24

Jesus wants us to pray about everything! Romans 12:12 tells us to "be joyful because you have hope. Be patient when trouble comes. Pray at all times" (ICB). We can trust that Jesus sees us and knows exactly what we need when we need it. Isn't that amazing? The God of creation sees *you* and knows exactly what you need right at this very moment. So we can be patient when things seem tough because we believe God will meet our needs. Philippians 4:19 promises, "My God will meet all your needs according to the riches of his glory in Christ Jesus" (NIV). But even though He already knows everything we need, He still wants us to keep talking to Him. Pray for Jesus to give you a clean heart and to show you where you've messed up, and thank Him for forgiving you. Talk to Jesus about all of your needs and thoughts. But also ask Him to care for those around you. Prayer changes things! The Bible tells us that when our hearts are right with God, our prayers are powerful and effective (James 5:16)!

God, thank You for hearing my prayers and meeting all of my needs. Even though You already know everything about me, I'm glad You still want to talk to me every day.

TAKE HOPE

"I have told you these things so you may have peace in Me.
In the world you will have much trouble. But take
hope! I have power over the world!"
JOHN 16:33

Life isn't easy. Not even when you're a kid. Growing up is hard work. Jesus understands! He had to grow up too! He is there for you, waiting to help you through every situation. He gives us tons of encouragement in His Word. Check these out:

- "Have I not commanded you? Be strong and courageous. Do not be afraid; do not be discouraged, for the LORD your God will be with you wherever you go." (Joshua 1:9 NIV)

- "It's a good thing to quietly hope, quietly hope for help from GOD. It's a good thing when you're young to stick it out through the hard times." (Lamentations 3:26–27 MSG)

- "For I am the LORD your God who takes hold of your right hand and says to you, Do not fear; I will help you." (Isaiah 41:13 NIV)

- "Since God assured us, 'I'll never let you down, never walk off and leave you,' we can boldly quote, God is there, ready to help; I'm fearless no matter what. Who or what can get to me?" (Hebrews 13:5–6 MSG)

Jesus, I'm so glad You understand my life! Thanks for helping me!

LOVING AND LIKING

"This is life that lasts forever. It is to know You, the only true
God, and to know Jesus Christ Whom You have sent."

JOHN 17:3

You have probably heard a lot about how much Jesus loves you in your
lifetime. But love and like are a little different, right? Do you think God
likes you? Zephaniah 3:17 says, "The LORD your God is with you, the
Mighty Warrior who saves. He will take great delight in you; in his love
he will no longer rebuke you, but will rejoice over you with singing" (NIV).
God likes you. It's true! He listens to your every word when you talk to
Him. And He *loves* you—even when you make mistakes. There's nothing
you could do to make Him love you more, and nothing you could do to
make Him love you less. When you come to know Jesus as your Savior,
God washes away all your sins, and He sees you as the perfect kid you
are. And you can say with confidence, "Jesus likes me!" He rejoices over
you, and the Bible says He even sings about you! You are liked. You are
loved. You are His!

---

*Jesus, You make my heart smile. Thank You for loving me—
and for liking me just the way I am. Thank You for seeing
me as perfect. I love You. I like You a whole lot too.*

THE JOY OF JESUS

"Now I come to You, Father. I say these things while I am in the
world. In this way, My followers may have My joy in their hearts."

JOHN 17:13

Jesus promised to fill us with His joy—and we don't have to wait until
heaven for that! Psalm 16:11 says, "You make known to me the path of
life; you will fill me with joy in your presence, with eternal pleasures at
your right hand" (NIV). We have access to Jesus' peace, joy, grace, and
presence right now while we live on earth through the power of the
Holy Spirit. Hebrews 4:15–16 encourages us too: "He's been through
weakness and testing, experienced it all—all but the sin. So let's walk
right up to him and get what he is so ready to give" (MSG). How cool is
that? Just "walk right up" to Jesus, and He will fill you with peace and joy
in His presence. Jesus is with you in this very moment. If you're having
trouble feeling joy in your life, get alone somewhere and talk to God. Tell
Him exactly how you feel, out loud, in your mind, or in a journal. Jesus
wants you to have joy in your heart. And if you don't, He will help!

Jesus, I ask that You would fill me with joy in Your presence.
I want Your constant presence in my life and
the joy that only You can give.

JESUS IN YOU

"I have made Your name known to them and will make
it known. So then the love You have for Me may
be in them and I may be in them."

JOHN 17:26

The disciples were sad that Jesus was going to leave them. John 17 is the prayer Jesus prayed for Himself, for His disciples, and for us. Yes, Jesus was praying for *you*! He prayed that the same love God the Father has for Him would be in you. Isn't that amazing? Jesus' disciples didn't understand that when Jesus went back to heaven, He would send His Spirit to live in our hearts. They didn't understand that Jesus would be alive in us. When Jesus was here on earth, He had limits because He was in a human body. He couldn't be everywhere at the same time. Now that He has risen and conquered death, His Spirit can be everywhere at once. The Bible tells us, "God decided to let his people know this rich and glorious truth which he has for all people. This truth is Christ himself, who is in you. He is our only hope for glory" (Colossians 1:27 ICB). Having Jesus alive inside of us is our only hope for the future.

*Jesus, thank You for praying for me! I'm amazed at how
much You love me. Let Your Spirit come alive
inside my heart so I can live for You.*

SENT

Then Jesus said to [His disciples] again, "May you have peace.
As the Father has sent Me, I also am sending you."

JOHN 20:21

Jesus has given us all work to do on this earth as we wait for Him to come back. He's given each of us gifts and talents to use to serve Him and share His love with others while we have the time. We want Jesus to tell us we've done a good job doing His work here. And when we've been faithful (being faithful means you do what you say you're going to do!) in doing certain tasks for God, He'll give us more and more tasks to finish. He'll continue to send us out. Humans easily lose interest in a job once they are stuck on a problem or bored with it. Finishing the job requires lots and lots of faithfulness. Finishing the job well requires lots of prayer and dependence on Jesus. Galatians 5:6 tells us, "The only thing that counts is faith expressing itself through love" (NIV). So if you're feeling tired and weak, remember that Jesus can be your strength for you. He can help you love like He loves. And that's the only thing that really counts.

Jesus, I ask that You would help me to be faithful in all the tasks that You give me on this earth. Help me not to lose hope when problems come but to finish the job well as I trust in You for help.

HAPPY TO BELIEVE

Jesus said to him, "Thomas, because you have seen Me, you believe.
Those are happy who have never seen Me and yet believe!"

JOHN 20:29

Thomas was one of Jesus' original twelve disciples. He was with Jesus during His ministry on earth and yet still had a hard time believing that Jesus rose from the dead. Even after witnessing the many miracles of Jesus firsthand! Grown-ups have a hard time believing in miracles sometimes. Jesus knew that Thomas needed to see His scars in order to believe, so He showed them to Thomas up close. Sometimes we wish we could see Jesus face-to-face just like Thomas. But did you catch what Jesus said to Thomas? "Those are happy who have never seen Me and yet believe." Jesus was talking about you and me and everyone who would come to believe in Him after He went back to heaven. He said we are happy and blessed because we have faith without actually seeing Him with our own eyes. What do you think He meant? *The Message* helps us understand a bit more: "You believe because you've seen with your own eyes. Even better blessings are in store for those who believe without seeing."

Jesus, help me believe even though I can't see. Increase my faith in
You, and help me to hear You speak to me through Your Word.
Thank You for blessing me! I'm happy to believe in You.

GOD'S WORD

Jesus did many other powerful works in front of His followers. They are not written in this book. But these are written so you may believe that Jesus is the Christ, the Son of God. When you put your trust in Him, you will have life that lasts forever through His name.

JOHN 20:30–31

Part of trusting Jesus is trusting in the truth of His Word. As believers we trust that the Bible is the inspired Word of God. Second Timothy 3:16 tells us what that means: "All Scripture is God-breathed and is useful for teaching, rebuking, correcting and training in righteousness" (NIV). How can we know the Bible is true? Don't be afraid to search out the truth for yourself. Many people have come to know Jesus by trying to prove the Bible wrong! The fact of the matter is this: the Word of God can be trusted. If you want to know how to live your life for God; if you need wisdom for today and hope for tomorrow; if you want to hear Jesus speak to you right now, get into God's Word. It will change your life!

Jesus, I want to believe in Your Word. Help me to know and understand what You are telling me in scripture. Thank You that I can know for sure that Your words are true!

ALIVE IN MANY WAYS

After [Jesus] had suffered much and then died, He showed Himself
alive in many sure ways for forty days. He told them
many things about the holy nation of God.

ACTS 1:3

Lee Strobel was an atheist—someone who doesn't believe in God. He
was also an investigative reporter for a large newspaper. After his wife
committed her life to Jesus, he wanted to prove that God was not real.
Through years of research and studying eye-witness accounts of what
happened while Jesus was alive, he came to the startling conclusion that
it would take *more faith* to believe that Jesus wasn't who He said He was
and to keep being an atheist! Did you catch that? He found that it would
take more faith on his part to keep believing that there was no God than
to accept the facts of history that Jesus is real, that He is God, and that
He rose from the dead! Not only is the Bible the inspired Word of God,
but it is a reliable historical textbook. You may have doubts about your
faith sometimes, and that's okay. It's what we do with our doubt that
matters. Jesus understands our doubts and questions. Ask Him to show
You how real He is. You'll be amazed at the way He shows up in your life!

Jesus, I want to believe You and trust You with my life.
Please help me see You in my world.

TO THE ENDS OF THE EARTH

"But you will receive power when the Holy Spirit comes into your life. You will tell about Me in the city of Jerusalem and over all the countries of Judea and Samaria and to the ends of the earth."

ACTS 1:8

If you're living your life to follow Jesus, other people are going to wonder about you! If you love Jesus and treat other people with kindness, you're going to get questions about why you do what you do. Are you ready to answer them? First Peter 3:15 tells us, "In your hearts revere Christ as Lord. Always be prepared to give an answer to everyone who asks you to give the reason for the hope that you have. But do this with gentleness and respect" (NIV). Some people may be unkind and make fun of you for being a Christian. Their words might make you angry. Before you answer them, ask for God's help. He is right there with you, and He sees everything that's happening. He wants you to answer with gentleness and respect, not anger and embarrassment. The reason they're asking is because they are looking for hope too! And they want to know if yours is real or not!

Jesus, help me remember that everyone else is looking for hope in You too. You created them that way. Help me to be gentle and respect others when I share my faith in You, to the ends of the earth.

CARRIED ON THE CLOUDS

When Jesus had said this and while they were still looking at Him, He was taken up. A cloud carried Him away so they could not see Him. They were still looking up to heaven, watching Him go. All at once two men dressed in white stood beside them. They said, "You men of the country of Galilee, why do you stand looking up into heaven? This same Jesus Who was taken from you into heaven will return in the same way you saw Him go up into heaven."

ACTS 1:9–11

Jesus spent a lot of time with His followers after He rose from the dead. He had a lot to share with them, and He wanted them to see that He was real, and that He really did conquer death. But it was time for Jesus to leave earth so He could send the Holy Spirit to us. Jesus was lifted up into the sky and went back to His rightful home in heaven. Two angels appeared and told Jesus' followers that Jesus would return in the same way He left, carried on the clouds. We are still waiting for that day when Jesus comes back. Jesus gave all of us assignments while we wait. Are you getting your heavenly homework done?

Jesus, please use my gifts and abilities to share the truth of who You are with the people You've put in my life. Fill me with Your Spirit so I can complete the work You've given me to do.

SPIRITUALLY ALIVE

"God says, 'In the last days I will send My Spirit on all men.
Then your sons and daughters will speak God's Word.
Your young men will see what God has given
them to see. Your old men will dream dreams.' "

ACTS 2:17

In the Old Testament, a prophet named Joel foretold that the Holy Spirit
would be sent to us many years before it actually happened. This was all
part of God's big plan to save His people. He knew we couldn't figure
out life alone. He knew we would need a helper to teach us and lead
us. So He sent His very own Spirit to live inside of us. Listen to this:
"Spiritually alive, we have access to everything God's Spirit is doing,
and can't be judged by unspiritual critics. Isaiah's question, 'Is there
anyone around who knows God's Spirit, anyone who knows what he is
doing?' has been answered: Christ knows, and we have Christ's Spirit"
(1 Corinthians 2:15–16 MSG). When we have the Spirit of Jesus alive
in us, we are being transformed, God's Word is brought to life in us, we
are able to understand things that we couldn't before, and we are taught
right and wrong. The ancient theologian Augustine said, "Without the
Spirit we can neither love God nor keep His commandments." The Holy
Spirit helps us to do both!

---

*Jesus, I'm happy that You sent me Your Spirit
to teach me and to help me follow You.*

THE SPIRIT'S WORK

"This Jesus has been lifted up to God's right side. The Holy Spirit was promised by the Father. God has given Him to us. That is what you are seeing and hearing now!"

ACTS 2:33

Corrie ten Boom was put in prison during World War II for helping Jews escape by hiding them in a closet in her home. She was a watchmaker and an author who learned to put her trust in Jesus. She said, "Trying to do the Lord's work in your own strength is the most confusing, exhausting, and tedious of all work. But when you are filled with the Holy Spirit, then the ministry of Jesus just flows out of you." Jesus promised to send us the Holy Spirit, and He did. But we have to accept the help of God's Spirit. He wants us to be filled with His Spirit to remind us of everything Jesus said. The Holy Spirit will remind us of how loved we are. He will help us hear from God. He will give us wisdom and lead us in the right direction. Jesus has special things for you to do, just as he had special things for Corrie ten Boom to do. Allow Him to fill you with His Spirit so that the ministry of Jesus will flow out of you too.

Jesus, I don't want to just work for You without Your help. Please fill me with Your Spirit.

THE PROMISE

Peter said to them, "Be sorry for your sins and turn from them
and be baptized in the name of Jesus Christ, and your sins will be
forgiven. You will receive the gift of the Holy Spirit. This promise
is to you and your children. It is to all people everywhere.
It is to as many as the Lord our God will call."

Acts 2:38-39

The men of Israel were listening as Peter shared about Jesus. Peter told them the whole story about how Jesus was put to death and rose from the dead. Then He went back to heaven and sent His Holy Spirit. The people were convicted. That means that they felt moved by the Holy Spirit and realized that the way they had been living was wrong. They asked what they could do to change. Peter told them that they needed to repent, which means to be sorry and turn from their sins. And then they were to be baptized. Peter went on to say that this promise was not just for the men of Israel who were listening that day; it's for us too. If we want to be like Jesus, we have to turn away from our bad choices and turn to God. Getting baptized shows others that you are serious about following Jesus. Ask your parents or church leaders for more information about getting baptized.

---

*Jesus, thank You for sending Your promised Holy Spirit
to help me turn away from bad choices and turn to You.*

EARLY MISSIONARIES

They were faithful in listening to the teaching of the missionaries.
They worshiped and prayed and ate the Lord's supper together.

ACTS 2:42

Jesus' disciples kept spreading the truth and love of Jesus, and the first Christian church was born. The Bible tells us that the new believers would gather together to eat and learn and worship Jesus. They shared everything and met one another's needs. God blessed them and kept adding to their numbers. Years later another missionary named Timothy was spreading God's Word. Paul, one of Jesus' followers, was teaching him. He said, "The purpose of my instruction is that all believers would be filled with love that comes from a pure heart, a clear conscience, and genuine faith" (1 Timothy 1:5 NLT). Paul's main goal as a missionary was that all believers would be filled with love from a pure heart, clear conscience, and real-life faith. Jesus Himself said that loving God and loving others is really all that matters. Paul repeated that message again and again. The Christian life is all about love from a pure heart. When it becomes more about rules and religion, that is not genuine faith in Jesus. God's hope for you as a young person is that you will be filled with purity and love. Ask Him to guard your heart.

Jesus, thank You that Your purpose for me is pure love.
Please guard my heart as I grow up. Fill me
with Your loving presence.

FAITH IN JESUS' NAME

"You see and know this man here. He has been made strong
through faith in Jesus' name. Yes, it is faith in Christ that
has made this man well and strong. This man is
standing here in front of you all."

ACTS 3:16

Through the power of the Holy Spirit, Peter healed a poor man who
had been crippled since he was born. The man jumped to his feet and
began praising God. All the people around were astonished and went
running to them. Peter asked them why they were all surprised at the
man's healing. Weren't they listening? Peter and John had been telling
them all about what Jesus had done and the power that was available to
those who believed. The crippled man was healed through faith in the
name of Jesus. Jesus' name is not to be used lightly. It's not a magic
word, and it should never be used in vain (that means we don't use His
name as a cuss word). There is power in the name of Jesus because Jesus
Himself gives the power. You can say the name of Jesus out loud as a
prayer anytime. Just remember that it's Jesus Himself hearing you call
His name. He's the One with the power.

---

*Jesus, help me to honor Your name and have faith
in the power of what You can do.*

REFRESHED

"You must be sorry for your sins and turn from them. You must
turn to God and have your sins taken away. Then many times
your soul will receive new strength from the Lord."

ACTS 3:19

Peter was still talking to the crowds who witnessed the healing of the
poor crippled man. He was telling them what they needed to do to be
saved. His message was the same as last time. To follow Jesus, you need
to turn away from bad choices and turn to Jesus. He says that when
you do this, refreshing times will come from God, and He will give you
new strength. Doesn't that sound good? Do you play any sports? Maybe
gymnastics or basketball? When you've worked hard on the court or the
mat, you can feel when your body needs to be refreshed. You need a drink
and a rest. Doesn't it feel so good to have a cold drink waiting for you as
you take a break? It gives you the energy to get up and finish the game.
Jesus wants to give us that kind of refreshment in our souls. Imagine
Him washing away your sins and refreshing you just like when you enjoy
a cool drink after working hard at sports. Then His Spirit gives you new
strength to get up and live for Him.

---

*Jesus, I want to turn away from poor choices and come to
You. Refresh me and wash my sins away. Fill me with
Your strength to live my life for You.*

HAVE YOU BEEN WITH JESUS?

They were surprised and wondered how easy it was for Peter
and John to speak. They could tell they were men who had not
gone to school. But they knew they had been with Jesus.

ACTS 4:13

One day after Jesus had gone back to heaven, Peter and John were speaking
to the people of Israel. They were obeying Jesus' command to go tell all
the world about Him. Peter and John weren't educated men. They were
fishermen. They were courageous because they knew Jesus personally. The
people knew by their words and actions that they must have been given
supernatural (special power from God) power. They could tell that Peter
and John had been with Jesus! Do you think people can tell when you've
been with Jesus? Years ago a youth pastor told his audience to "get so
close to God that you smell like Him"! How is that even possible? How
can an invisible God be close to us? In Psalm 73:28 the psalmist wrote,
"It is good to be near God. I have made the Sovereign LORD my refuge"
(NIV). A refuge is a safe place. It's where you go for protection, relief, and
escape. When you make Jesus your refuge, it means you go to Him for
everything. You talk to Him about everything and listen for His answers.

---

*Jesus, I can't see the wind, but I know it's there—just like
You. Remind me that You're always near. Help me
come to You for everything.*

SHARE EVERYTHING

The many followers acted and thought the same way.
None of them said that any of their things were
their own, but they shared all things.

ACTS 4:32

The early church took care of its people. The Bible tells us that they didn't have a needy person among them. If someone was sick or needed food or had a need of any kind, the other Christians sold their possessions to help. They didn't consider anything they owned to be off-limits. They realized that everything they had was a gift from God. And God blessed them even more for that. How do you feel about your stuff? Do you realize that everything you have is a gift and a blessing from God? Is there a way that you could bless someone in your community who doesn't have as much as you? Get together with your family and discuss ways that you can help with needs in your community. Maybe you can start a money jar to bless someone at Christmastime. What if out of every dollar you earn, you put a little bit aside to help someone else? You could also consider sponsoring a child in need who lives in another country. Have your parents help research opportunities to share. Proverbs 11:25 in *The Message* says, "The one who blesses others is abundantly blessed; those who help others are helped."

Jesus, please open opportunities for my family to share
what we have with other people who have less.

GOD OR MAN?

Then Peter and the missionaries said,
"We must obey God instead of men!"
ACTS 5:29

Jesus' followers were under attack, just like Jesus had warned them. They were on trial for spreading the Gospel of Jesus to everyone who would listen after having been told by the authorities to stop. But Jesus' followers knew the truth and the power of God—and they would not be stopped. They knew that they had to obey Jesus instead of these authorities. Sometimes in life people will start acting big and God might start feeling small. Grown-ups and teachers and friends might all be telling you one thing, but you know in your heart that Jesus wants you to do something else. Certain people's approval of you might seem pretty important. You want your teacher or coach or friends to like you. But it's much more important to please Jesus than it is to please a person. Ask Him, and He will give you the strength to say the right thing at the right time and to do what He is asking you to do. If God is feeling too small to you and people seem too big, tell Jesus how you feel. Jesus gave His disciples courage and power through His Spirit to stand up for their faith even under severe attack. He will help you too.

Jesus, sometimes I'm confused. I need Your help to know what to say and do. I want to please You, not other people.

THE GOSPEL SPREADS

"I say to you now, stay away from these men and leave them alone.
If this teaching and work is from men, it will come to nothing.
If it is from God, you will not be able to stop it. You may
even find yourselves fighting against God."

ACTS 5:38–39

The early church was severely persecuted for spreading the Gospel of Jesus. To be persecuted means that cruel things were done to them because of what they stood for. A Jewish leader told the crowd to stop persecuting the first missionaries. He reminded them that if the teachings of Jesus were real, no man would be able to stop them. And if they weren't real, nothing would happen and they would eventually stop. As you know, the teachings of Jesus are real and the Gospel has been spread over the earth for close to two thousand years! No man or government has been able to stop the spread of the Gospel, even though many have tried. One historical leader tried to burn every copy of the Bible. And in some places and times, being a Christian has been against the law. It is a miracle from God that we know about Jesus and have His Words to read today. Jesus said, "Heaven and earth will pass away, but my words will never pass away" (Matthew 24:35 NIV).

Jesus, I am so thankful that I know You
and have Your words to read!

THE FRUIT OF BEING LIKE JESUS

The fruit that comes from having the Holy Spirit in our lives is:
love, joy, peace, not giving up, being kind, being good, having faith,
being gentle, and being the boss over our own desires.

GALATIANS 5:22–23

We've been reading the Gospels together to learn how to be more like Jesus. When the Spirit of God is at work in your heart, He produces fruit. If you are becoming like Jesus, you will have fruit growing in your life right now. Philippians 1:9–11 says, "I pray that your love will overflow more and more, and that you will keep on growing in knowledge and understanding. For I want you to understand what really matters, so that you may live pure and blameless lives until the day of Christ's return. May you always be filled with the fruit of your salvation—the righteous character produced in your life by Jesus Christ—for this will bring much glory and praise to God" (NLT). Can you see love, joy, peace, patience, kindness, goodness, faithfulness, gentleness, and self-control taking root and expanding in your heart? If you can, this brings much glory to God! If you're not sure, start talking to Jesus about it. Ask Him to clear out your heart to make room for what He wants to plant there.

*Jesus, please fill me up with the fruit of Your Spirit.
I want to see You at work in my life.*

A LIFE OF LOVE

We have come to know and believe the love God has for us.
God is love. If you live in love, you live by the
help of God and God lives in you.

1 JOHN 4:16

Love is the first fruit of the Spirit that is mentioned. Did you know that the biblical definition of love is God? God = love. Love = God. This world has a really messed-up view of love. Most people think love is a feeling of happiness, but that's not always true. Love is a choice. You can choose to love someone even if you don't feel like it. First Corinthians 13:4–8 tells us a little bit more of what true love is like: "Love is patient, love is kind. It does not envy, it does not boast, it is not proud. It does not dishonor others, it is not self-seeking, it is not easily angered, it keeps no record of wrongs. Love does not delight in evil but rejoices with the truth. It always protects, always trusts, always hopes, always perseveres. Love never fails" (NIV). That's a lot different than the way movies paint it, right? When you choose a life of love, it won't always be easy. It means you're always seeking the heart of Jesus instead of your own. And He will bless you abundantly for it!

---

*Jesus, please help me to choose love for You and
others instead of choosing my own way.*

LOVING-KINDNESS

The Lord will finish the work He started for me.
O Lord, Your loving-kindness lasts forever.
PSALM 138:8

The love Jesus has for you is unfailing and faithful. He is with you always. He is listening, and He loves you like you're the only kid in the universe! You are His child, and He will never abandon you. You are a child of the King of all kings, and He has wonderful plans for your life. Even the painful things that happen in life, God will miraculously turn into good things if you trust in Him (Romans 8:28 again—you should definitely know this verse by now!). Philippians 1:6 tells us, "I am certain that God, who began the good work within you, will continue his work until it is finally finished on the day when Christ Jesus returns" (NLT). As you grow up, you're going to have a lot of distractions in life as the enemy tries to get you to turn away from trusting in God's great love for you. Satan's one purpose is to distract you and separate you from God. So remember how much Jesus loves you, and hide His Words in your heart. Memorize scripture and allow the Holy Spirit to bring it to your mind anytime you start to forget.

God, I pray that You would keep me from getting too distracted in this life. I want to follow You. Thank You for Your loving-kindness and the great plans You have for me.

JOY IN A NEW DAY

Crying may last for a night, but joy comes with the new day.
PSALM 30:5

Joy is the second fruit of the Spirit mentioned in Galatians 5:22–23. We've talked a lot about joy, but today let's talk about having joy when life is hard. The Bible reminds us again and again that there are different seasons in life. Just like we have winter, spring, summer, and fall—each bringing something new and necessary to our world—we also have different seasons of life. God's Word tells us that "there is a time for everything, and a season for every activity under the heavens" (Ecclesiastes 3:1 NIV). You may be in a hard season of life right now, going through a lot of changes. But always remember, it's just a season. As the saying goes, "This too shall pass." That means that though things might be hard right now, another day will come—a fresh new day without the same troubles that today had. Allow these thoughts to bring you comfort. The hard stuff might last for a season, but joy is just around the corner.

Jesus, please help me to get through hard days, knowing that this is only a season and that You offer constant peace and joy in Your presence. Thank You for the different seasons of my life. Use them to make me more like You.

JOY AND TROUBLES

Dear friends, your faith is going to be tested as if it were going through fire. Do not be surprised at this. Be happy that you are able to share some of the suffering of Christ. When His shining-greatness is shown, you will be filled with much joy.

1 PETER 4:12–13

Life in a messed-up world can be difficult. Jesus Himself told us we're going to have trouble here, so we should expect it. Remember that He also said, "Take heart! I have overcome the world" (John 16:33 NIV). How can we live with joy in our hearts while we're expecting trouble? Well, we wake up each morning expecting some challenges, and we ask Jesus to help us through each and every one. You may wake up and pray, "Jesus, I know that I'm going to have some problems today. But instead of getting grumpy or being afraid, I will take Your hand and let You help me through this day." We don't have to be sad or afraid, expecting the worst. Always look at trouble as a challenge that can be conquered with the power of Jesus. When trouble comes we are sharing in the sufferings of Jesus Christ—and that is a powerful thing. We can find Jesus in each trial, and He will give us joy in His presence!

Jesus, I'm expecting some challenges today, and I know You will be with me through them all. Please give me Your power and wisdom to get through each one.

PEACE AND A WONDERFUL LIFE

Our hope comes from God. May He fill you with joy and peace
because of your trust in Him. May your hope grow
stronger by the power of the Holy Spirit.

ROMANS 15:13

Peace is the third fruit of the Spirit listed in Galatians. Think of a person you know who loves Jesus with their whole heart and seeks to follow Him in everything they do. Do you know anyone like that? Ask Jesus to bring a specific person to your mind. Is there a special light in their eyes and an unshakable hope in their heart? Jesus can fill you with that very same kind of peace and joy. When you commit to follow Jesus, the God of all hope changes you. Can you imagine watching a movie where nothing bad or challenging ever happened? Where the main characters didn't have to overcome any problems? That would probably be a pretty boring show. In good times and bad, you can still overflow with hope and peace because of the power of the Holy Spirit living inside of You. This makes life wonderful and worth living—even during difficult times. Pray to the God of hope and ask Him to fill you to overflowing. He will do it!

*Jesus, thank You for giving me this wonderful life. Light up my eyes
and my soul with Your joy and peace. Let others see the
difference in me so that I can point them to You.*

STRENGTH AND PEACE

The Lord will give strength to His people.
The Lord will give His people peace.

PSALM 29:11

The Bible tells us that Jesus gives us His strength and peace. Peace is impossible to find on our own. When we obey God by being thankful and not worrying, He gives us true and lasting peace. Psalm 34:14–15 says, "Turn away from evil and do good. Search for peace, and work to maintain it. The eyes of the LORD watch over those who do right; his ears are open to their cries for help" (NLT). We have to keep giving our worries to Jesus and replacing them with thankfulness every single day. And if we want Jesus to watch over us and hear our prayers, we have to keep away from evil and do good. The Bible says that we need to turn away from evil, to actually stop and go the other direction. But even then we can't just assume that trouble won't find us if we're not looking for it. Our enemy is constantly looking for ways to get us to turn away from God (1 Peter 5:8) so that our peace is destroyed. Ask Jesus to help you turn and go the other way so you can keep your eyes on Him.

Jesus, please fill me with Your strength and peace.
Please help me to turn away from evil and to seek You in all things.

TROUBLES BRING PATIENCE

We are glad for our troubles also. We know that
troubles help us learn not to give up.
ROMANS 5:3

Patience is the fourth fruit of the Spirit listed in Galatians 5:22–23. Has anyone ever asked you to have some patience? Patience can be a difficult fruit to grow. When you're going through hard times, it's easy to get discouraged. You want things to change, and you want them to change quickly! Sometimes it can be really hard to keep a good attitude when you need things to change so badly. But hard times can actually be really good for us if we allow God to work in them. *The Message* says it this way: "We continue to shout our praise even when we're hemmed in with troubles, because we know how troubles can develop passionate patience in us" (Romans 5:3). While it's definitely hard to be glad for trouble, we learn to trust Jesus more in those times, and hard times teach us to be patient too. We learn not to give up. Hard times give us an opportunity to trust God's Word. We remember Romans 8:28 again, and we patiently trust God to bring good out of bad.

---

*Jesus, I know I can give You praise and thank You even during
hard times. I trust Your Word, and I choose to wait patiently
and watch with great expectation while You turn
these bad things into good life lessons.*

BE STILL AND WAIT

Rest in the Lord and be willing to wait for Him. Do not trouble
yourself when all goes well with the one who
carries out his sinful plans.

PSALM 37:7

"Be still and wait"—those are some of the hardest words for us to hear
and sometimes nearly impossible for us to do, it seems! But Jesus wants
us to come before Him and wait patiently as He does His will in our lives.
He tells us not to worry when bad things happen, because He will make
all things right. In fact, Jesus said, "It is finished!" as He was hanging on
the cross for us (John 19:30). That means that death and sin have already
been conquered forever! They have no hold on us. Bad people might do
bad things and seem to get away with them for now, but God sees all
things, and everything is in His hands. So the next time someone does
something mean to you on purpose, go straight to Jesus and be still. Tell
Jesus how you feel about it. Don't take out your own revenge. Just wait
patiently for God to take care of it. It sounds hard, but Jesus will give
you the strength to do things His way. Rest in the Lord, and be willing
to wait for Him.

---

*Jesus, please give me the strength to take matters to You
instead of taking them into my own hands.
Help me to be patient and wait for You.*

KINDNESS

O man, He has told you what is good. What does the Lord ask
of you but to do what is fair and to love kindness,
and to walk without pride with your God?

MICAH 6:8

Kindness is the fifth fruit of the Spirit listed in Galatians. In the Old
Testament book of Micah, the people of Israel continued to disobey
God. They were making really bad choices—even building altars to false
gods! But God was still kind and patient with them. He used a prophet
named Micah to remind them of what He wanted them to do. Micah
spoke to the people and told them that God wanted them to do justice
(to be fair in all of their ways), to be kind, and to walk humbly with God.
God is good, and all His ways are good. And He wants us to follow Him
by making those same kinds of choices. Know that every time you treat
someone else with kindness, you bless that person. And that person may
go on to bless someone else, and they bless someone else, and on and on!

Jesus, please help me to walk with You each day in a way
that makes You smile! Help me to be fair and kind,
just like You! Help me to be humble too.

PURSUING KINDNESS AND RIGHTEOUSNESS

The man who shows loving-kindness does himself good,
but the man without pity hurts himself.
PROVERBS 11:17

Kindness is a pretty simple act. Most of us understand how to be kind and that everyone likes to be treated with kindness. Proverbs 21:21 says, "Whoever pursues righteousness and kindness will find life, righteousness, and honor" (ESV). Kindness is a simple process to think about, but do you actually pursue it? Pursuing righteousness means seeking God's approval (Philippians 3:9). And we can't do that on our own. The only way to receive God's approval is through accepting what Jesus did for us on the cross and living for Him. And when we've done that, God looks at us and sees us through Jesus! That means He sees us as perfect, and nothing we could ever do or not do could make Him love us any more than He already does! Think about that today. And if you want to find life, righteousness, and honor, live for Jesus and act out of kindness. Remember, one act of kindness passed on and on and on can change the world!

---

*Jesus, thank You again and again for Your great love for me.
I'm so thankful that You took away all of my sin—past,
present, and future. Help me to pursue Your
righteousness and kindness to share with others.*

GOODNESS

Turn from sin, and do good, so you will live forever.
PSALM 37:27

Goodness is the sixth fruit of the Spirit mentioned in Galatians 5:22–23. When we confess our sins to Jesus and receive His forgiveness, the next step is for us to turn away from the sin we've been doing. He already knows what you've done, but He wants to talk with you about it. He wants to help you through it and give you peace. We can't pretend that sin will just go away on its own. It takes action on our part. And we can't find goodness on our own either—we have to let the Spirit of God plant and grow goodness inside of us. As humans we still make big mistakes from time to time. First John 1:9 says, "If we confess our sins, [God] is faithful and just and will forgive us our sins and purify us from all unrighteousness" (NIV). When you've messed up big, turn back to Jesus and start to trust Him again—to *really* trust Him. When you trust Jesus with everything you have, He gives you the ability to do good and to be faithful. His power is alive and at work within you.

Jesus, please keep me from evil and plant goodness in my heart.
I want to do Your will and bring glory and honor to You.

FAITHFULNESS

I will sing of the loving-kindness of the Lord forever. I will make known with my mouth how faithful You are to all people.

PSALM 89:1

Faithfulness is the seventh fruit of the Spirit that Jesus wants to grow in your heart. No one on this earth can be completely faithful to you all the time. Not your parents, not your best friend, not people you trust from church—no one gets it right all the time. Your parents will try their best, of course. But even parents sometimes forget to do something they said they would do. No one is completely faithful, that is, except Jesus. And Jesus directs all His love and faithfulness right toward you. He will never leave you. He'll never give up on you. He'll never lie to you. He'll never ever stop loving you. Nothing you could do will ever change His mind about how much He loves you. That's a big deal! The biggest! God looks at you and smiles because He sees Jesus in you. God is your loving Parent who never gets it wrong. You don't have to be afraid to talk to Him or tell Him what's going on in your life. He already knows, and He wants to hear from you.

Jesus, I want to know more about You, and I want to grow closer to You each day. Thank You for Your amazing love and faithfulness to me.

KEEPING THE FAITH

"God clothes the grass of the field. It lives today and is burned
in the stove tomorrow. How much more will He
give you clothes? You have so little faith!"
MATTHEW 6:30

Our enemy loves to distract us and get us to worry. When we worry, our focus is never on Jesus, so the enemy wins. Fear and worry are signs that we aren't trusting Jesus very much. It means that Jesus is very small in our lives and our faith is small. So what can be done about that? Go to Jesus and confess your lack of faith. When people and things are big in your life, Jesus doesn't have the room He needs to be big in your world. And that means there are idols in your heart. Anything that comes between you and God—whether it's good or bad—is an idol. Maybe it's someone you love, and that person's opinion of you matters more than Jesus' opinion. Or maybe your desire for something is so great that it is getting in the way of what Jesus wants to do in your life. Bring these things to Jesus and allow Him to increase your faith. God's Word gives us this encouragement: "If you don't know what you're doing, pray to the Father. He loves to help. You'll get his help, and won't be condescended to when you ask for it. Ask boldly, believingly, without a second thought" (James 1:5–6 MSG).

God, please remove any idols in my heart.
I want You to be big in my life!

GENTLENESS

A gentle answer turns away anger,
but a sharp word causes anger.
PROVERBS 15:1

Gentleness is the eighth fruit of the Spirit listed in Galatians 5:22–23. Being gentle is important to Jesus, so it needs to be important to us as well. Proverbs 15:4 tells us, "Gentle words are a tree of life; a deceitful tongue crushes the spirit" (NLT). You can use words for good or for evil. Do you know anyone who loves to argue? Maybe you've seen someone on TV who always wants to get their own way, and they argue with anyone who says differently. When one person is yelling at another, it stirs up anger in the other person. Then the arguing gets louder and louder and angrier and angrier. But answering someone with gentleness can turn off their anger. And if it doesn't, you can just walk away. Proverbs 29:11 says, "Fools vent their anger, but the wise quietly hold it back" (NLT). Wise people take their thoughts to Jesus first before sharing them with someone else. Francis de Sales said, "Nothing is so strong as gentleness, nothing so gentle as real strength."

---

*Jesus, help me to be strong and gentle at the same time.
Please give me Your strength as I face anyone who may be
angry in the future. Help me to answer gently or to walk away.*

SELF-CONTROL

No temptation has overtaken you except what is common to
mankind. And God is faithful; he will not let you be tempted
beyond what you can bear. But when you are tempted,
he will also provide a way out so that you can endure it.

1 CORINTHIANS 10:13 NIV

Self-control is the last fruit of the Spirit mentioned in Galatians 5:22–23. We don't hear a lot about self-control today, but it is important to Jesus. Second Peter 1:5–7 tells us, "Make every effort to add to your faith goodness; and to goodness, knowledge; and to knowledge, self-control; and to self-control, perseverance; and to perseverance, godliness; and to godliness, mutual affection; and to mutual affection, love" (NIV). This list actually shows more of the characteristics that Jesus wants to plant and grow in your life. As you continue growing in Jesus, more and more fruit will grow too. Our enemy, Satan, is out to trip up young people in any way he can. He often aims his arrows right at your self-control, trying to get you to do things you know are wrong and impure. Ask Jesus to fill you up with His power to overcome all the tricks of the enemy. Memorize 1 Corinthians 10:13. Jesus always provides a way out of temptation!

---

*Jesus, please help me to look for the escape routes You put in
my path every time I'm tempted to do wrong. I know
You are bigger and stronger than the enemy.*

BE SUNSHINE

At one time you lived in darkness. Now you are living
in the light that comes from the Lord. Live as children
who have the light of the Lord in them.

EPHESIANS 5:8

Do you know anybody who looks like sunshine? You know, when they walk into the room it's almost like the whole place lights up? Jesus said, "I am the light of the world. Whoever follows me will never walk in darkness, but will have the light of life" (John 8:12 NIV). When we follow Jesus, He fills us up with His very own light. It's the light of life that makes believers shine from the inside out—kind of like sunshine! After a long, cold winter, there's nothing like walking out into the sunshine come spring. The sun makes us feel warm, and we actually need the vitamin D the sun provides to be healthy! Ask Jesus to make you into living sunshine. Ask Him to fill You with His light so that others feel warm and healthy when they are around you. You have an amazing opportunity every day to make a difference in the lives of everyone you see. At school, at church, at the library, at the mall, at a restaurant—everywhere. The only smile that person might see the whole day could be from you. Be like Jesus—go be His light in a dark world.

Jesus, help me light up this dark world
with the sunshine of Your love.

ABOUT THE AUTHOR

MariLee Parrish is the author of many books and devotionals for women and families. She makes her home in Colorado with her husband and two children. Visit marileeparrish.com for more information.